Justice Thomas Berger, commissioner of Mackenzie Valley Pipeline Inquiry, conducts outdoor community hearing at Slavey community of Nahanni Butte, N.W.T.
(Courtesy of Canapress Photo Service, News of the North)

Comparative Ethics Series/
Collection d'Éthique Comparée : 3

Comparative Ethics Series/
Collection d'Éthique Comparée

As Religious Studies in its various branches has spread out in recent years, it has met with a newly emergent discipline: Comparative Ethics as the study of moralities as cultural systems, rather than as the philosophical investigation of particular moral issues. To study a morality as a dynamic whole in its social nature and functioning requires a context in which other instances of a comparable kind are considered. Moral action-guides and religious action-guides have historically been brought together in mixed, moral-religious or religious-moral systems. The different paths followed by moralities as cultural systems in the varying contexts demand comparative study.

The series embraces three kinds of studies: (1) methodological studies, which will endeavour to elaborate and discuss principles, concepts, and models for the new discipline; (2) studies which aim at deepening our knowledge of the nature and functioning, the scope and content of particular moral systems, such as the Islamic, the Hindu, the Christian, and so on; (3) studies of a directly comparative kind, which bring differing moral systems or elements of systems into relationship.

COMPARATIVE ETHICS

Volume 3

Prophets, Pastors and Public Choices

Canadian Churches and the Mackenzie Valley Pipeline Debate

Roger Hutchinson

Published for the Canadian Corporation for Studies in Religion/Corporation Canadienne des Sciences Religieuses by Wilfrid Laurier University Press

1992

Canadian Cataloguing in Publication Data

Hutchinson, Roger, 1935-
  Prophets, pastors and public choices

(Comparative ethics series ; v. 3)
Includes bibliographical references and index.
ISBN 0-88920-207-9

1. Mackenzie Valley Pipeline (N.W.T.) — Moral and
ethical aspects. 2. Mackenzie Valley Pipeline
(N.W.T.) — Environmental aspects. 3. Church and social
problems — Canada. I. Canadian Corporation for
Studies in Religion. II. Title. III. Series.

BV4404.C2H8 1992   262.8'3628   C92-093360-2

© 1992 Canadian Corporation for Studies in Religion/
     Corporation Canadienne des Sciences Religieuses

Cover design by Connolly Design Inc.

Cover stock recycled paper

Printed in Canada

Prophets, Pastors and Public Choices: Canadian Churches and the Mackenzie Valley Pipeline Debate has been produced from a manuscript supplied in camera-ready form by the author.

Cover photograph: Rosie Albert interpreting for furskin trapper Jim Koe at
                  Ingamo Hall, Inuvik, February 1976
                        (Courtesy of Canapress Photo Service, Diana Crosbie)

Order from:
WILFRID LAURIER UNIVERSITY PRESS
Waterloo, Ontario, Canada N2L 3C5

Contents

List of Illustrations

Project North at General Council

It was moved by Rev. D. Lewis, seconded by Rev. P. Cline and agreed, that in view of the introductory statement of the Division of Mission in Canada regarding the overview of its work, this General Council affirm the position of the Division of Mission in Canada of a dual concern for and emphasis on both its prophetic and pastoral mission to all people of the North.

*— 1977 General Council of the
United Church of Canada*

Acknowledgements

It is perhaps a fitting use of the image to say that this study of the Mackenzie Valley pipeline debate has been in the pipeline for more years than I care to count. Like Nellie McClung, I will neither apologize nor explain. I will, rather, acknowledge some of my more obvious debts and urge readers to explore for themselves the relevance of this study of the pipeline debate of the mid-seventies for understanding and dealing with conflicting perspectives on complex issues of public policy.

I am grateful for the research grants from the Social Sciences and Humanities Research Council which enabled me to hire research assistants and to cover other research expenses. Brian Ruttan, Ron Sawatsky and Randi Warne located and collected relevant documents, conducted interviews and helped me to discover the focus which would end up characterizing the study. Murray Angus provided me with far more documentation and analysis of federal government northern development and native land claims policies than I was able to incorporate into the study. Geoffrey Johnston's study of the theological ideas of inter-church coalition staff provided useful background for my reflections on the theological debate within each church.

Quotations from *Northern Frontier, Northern Homeland: The Report of the Mackenzie Valley Pipeline Inquiry*, vol. 1, have been supplied by the Privy Council Office and are reproduced with the permission of the Minister of Supply and Services Canada, 1992. Quotations from *Northern Development: The Canadian Dilemma* are used by permission of the Canadian publishers, McClelland & Stewart, Toronto.

Although I must assume full responsibility for the final shape of this study, and for the interpretations and judgments contained in it, I received a great deal of help along the way. An early consultation with Terry Anderson, Patrick Hartt, Pat Kerans, Robert Page and Gibson Winter was particularly useful. Tony Clarke, Karmel Taylor-McCullum and Menno Wiebe gave generously of their time as my formal contacts with the Project North Administrative Committee. The many other persons on both sides of the debate who shared their views freely with my research assistants and me helped me to keep in mind the complex persons behind the arguments I have attempted to analyze.

As the manuscript approached completion, other debts were incurred. Financial assistance from a Lilly Endowment, Inc. faculty development grant administered by the Emmanuel College Centre for the Study of Religion in Canada enabled me to leave final preparation of the manuscript in Heather Gamester's capable hands. Sandra Woolfrey and Maura Brown of WLU Press provided careful guidance and friendly advice at each crucial stage. I would also like to thank Charles Davis, editor of the Comparative Ethics Series, for his encouragement and insightful support; William James, Jack Lightstone and David Jobling, some of whose terms on the Corporation's Publications Committee this project has outlived; the anonymous readers for the Canadian Federation for the Humanities, whose criticisms forced me both to say more clearly what I was trying to say and to think again about some aspects of my approach; and my wife and sons, who were constant and patient in their support. The book is dedicated to Moira, Tim and Alex.

This book has been published with the help of a grant from the Canadian Federation for the Humanities, using funds provided by the Social Sciences and Humanities Research Council of Canada.

Introduction

This analysis of the Mackenzie Valley pipeline debate is a case study in comparative ethics. As an introduction to the genre, aim and scope of the study I will first consider how the method I am using in this study relates to other approaches to the discipline of comparative ethics. Next, an "objective" account of the main events and final outcome of the pipeline debate will be given, even though one of the aims of the case study is to challenge the usefulness of the sharp distinction which is often made between "objective" claims about facts and "subjective" value judgments. Finally, I will explain my interest in the role of the Canadian churches, and provide a very brief history of Project North. This inter-church coalition was created in the fall of 1975 by the Anglican, Roman Catholic and United churches. Its main purpose was to help the churches to be more effective allies of the native peoples, whose cry for justice they believed deserved to be heard more clearly by southern Canadians.

1. Comparative Ethics and Christian Social Ethics

Comparative ethics has fairly recently emerged as a subdiscipline within religious studies.[1] It is most commonly associated with comparative historical studies of religious traditions, especially traditions other than Christianity;[2] or with philosophical and sociological studies designed to produce precise categories for the cross-cultural study of morality and religion.[3] In addition, however, a heightened interest in comparative ethics has accompanied developments during the past two decades in philosophical ethics[4] and in Christian social ethics. My own interest in becoming more explicitly comparative is related to my experiences as a teacher in a department of religious studies and a theological college, to my involvement in the social justice work of the churches, and to the developments in Christian and religious social ethics to which I have referred.

As an instructor in a university course on contemporary problems in religious ethics, I found it relatively easy to adapt my approach to a religious studies setting in which not all students shared my Christian, and particularly my United Church, identity. It was more difficult, however, to do justice to the perspectives of students whose assumptions about individual freedom, religious authority and so forth differed from the "situation ethics" approach which was in vogue among liberal Protestants when I started teaching. From the standpoint

1

of Roman Catholic, conservative Protestant and Orthodox Jewish students, situation ethics reflected my liberal Protestant outlook rather than a theologically neutral stance. The desire to be non-confessional, that is, to avoid providing instruction in a particular faith, was a necessary but insufficient response to the religious diversity I discovered in my classrooms. It was necessary to become more self-consciously comparative, both at the levels of factual claims and ethical arguments and at the level of interpretative frameworks.

In 1985 I switched from the Victoria College Department of Religious Studies to Emmanuel College, the United Church member of the Toronto School of Theology. My experiences with United Church students from different backgrounds, as well as with students from the other TST colleges, has reinforced my conviction that it is also necessary to be explicitly comparative regarding differences within particular denominations as well as among traditions. Contrary to the fears of some colleagues, this willingness to deal more explicitly with differences in spirituality, theology and political positions makes us more rather than less interested in the nature and roles of our spiritualities and theologies.[5]

As I became more sensitive to religious diversity in the classroom I also became more interested in the way conflicting positions on issues ranging from abortion and homosexuality to northern pipelines were being handled within particular churches or in ecumenical settings, such as the recently created inter-church social action coalitions. Just as in nineteenth- century Canada Lord Durham found two nations warring within the bosom of a single state, in relation to the pipeline debate I observed different Christian factions warring within the bosom of each church. It struck me that it seemed easier to achieve open and undistorted communication among representatives of different religious traditions, or different Christian denominations, than it was among members of a particular church. I became intrigued by the possibility that the protocols and categories developed for cross-cultural studies and inter-faith and ecumenical dialogue could be applied to debates within a particular religious group. As I demonstrated in a preliminary fashion in "Comparative Ethics and the Mackenzie Valley Pipeline Debate," my approach to the clarification of the pipeline debate involves treating different groups within the churches as if they belonged to different religious traditions. That is, the general orientation, norms and substantive judgments of one group are not presumed to be normative for all factions within a particular denomination.[6]

Even when one aims to take a comparative approach and to respect the different experiences, factual claims, ethical arguments and interpretative frameworks of various participants in a debate, a number of factors will influence which data are gathered, how the various claims and counterclaims are organized and interpreted, and what judgments are made about different positions.[7] Different emphases within comparative ethics can be mapped in relation to two types of tension. One type of tension is between what I will call "pragmatic" and "foundationalist" approaches. A second type of tension, which was a central feature of the methodological debates of the Religious Social Ethics Group of the American Academy of Religion, is between "engagement" and "detachment."[8] These admittedly crude polarities, which can be pictured as intersecting axes, will be used for the limited purpose of locating myself in relation to different strands of the subdiscipline.

Foundationalism is often used as a term of abuse by critics of academic philosophers who make exaggerated claims about their own rationality and who imply that persons who disagree with them are being subjective or emotional. It is therefore important to be clear about what I mean by the term.

As I am using the term, foundationalism refers to the strand of Enlightenment thinking which, according to Alasdair MacIntyre, had as its central aspiration the desire "to provide for debate in the public realm standards and methods of rational justification by which alternative courses of action in every sphere of life could be adjudged just or unjust, rational or irrational, enlightened or unenlightened."[9] It was the hope of Enlightenment thinkers and their successors, such as the authors of the *Encyclopédie*, Rousseau, Bentham, Kant and the Scottish philosophers of commonsense and their French and American disciples, that "reason would displace authority and tradition." As MacIntyre points out, "Rational justification was to appeal to principles undeniable by any rational person and therefore independent of all those social and cultural particularities which the Enlightenment thinkers took to be the mere accidental clothing of reason in particular times and places."[10]

What I will call soft foundationalism involves the claim that there are "principles . . . which would be found undeniable by all rational persons."[11] Hard foundationalism, on the other hand, links this claim about the existence of rationally binding principles with the further claim outlined above regarding methods of rational justification. It is the claim that there are "standards and methods of rational justification by which alternative courses of action in every sphere of life could be adjudged just or unjust . . . independent of all those social and cultural particularities" which gives the impression that actual judgments can be deduced from first principles. Not surprisingly, some ethicists adopt the opposite extreme. They start with concrete issues and actual cases and show how judgments are inferred from practical knowledge of particular situations. Their approach is inductive rather than deductive, and their interests are pragmatic rather than foundational.[12]

Pragmatists such as Jeffrey Stout are not as concerned to deny the presence in our language of rationally binding principles as they are to present an alternative understanding of the moral life and the nature of practical moral reasoning. I will use recent exchanges among David Little, Sumner Twiss, Ronald Green and Jeffrey Stout to illustrate the tension between foundationalists and pragmatists.

When I read Little and Twiss' 1978 *Comparative Religious Ethics*, Green's 1978 *Religious Reason* and Stout's 1981 *The Flight from Authority*, I recall thinking that they were each addressing different aspects of the moral life and thus making complementary contributions to the discipline. I realized that my own basic assumptions and interests were most adequately expressed by Stout, but it did not seem necessary to choose among Green's Kantian rationalism; Stout's holistic, pragmatic, historicist approach; or Little and Twiss' middle way between an "apples and oranges" rejection of comparative work and "grand theory" approaches which abstract from the rich cultural diversity of different traditions.[13] However, the session devoted to Stout's new book at the 1990 meetings of the Society of Christian Ethics made it appear as if the authors thought that such a choice was necessary.[14]

Green claims that Stout's refusal to look for justifying grounds beyond "the available moral materials of a culture" leaves him with

> no moral resources beyond those present within any particular culture for evaluating moral arguments. Nor does he offer any procedures, even within a culture, for morally assessing the variety of edifices that various do-it-yourselfers might choose to erect. If ethics is the effort to develop objective and rational standards for evaluating moral arguments, *Ethics after Babel* has no ethics. Worse, it systematically disempowers efforts to develop one.[15]

Stout accepted the truth of Green's conditional phrase, and agreed that "*If* we accept Ron's definition of ethics, *then* my book is not ethics." He did not, of course, accept Green's definition of ethics. "Why accept a definition of ethics that marginalizes Aristotle's ethics, that includes Kurt Baier but excludes Annette Baier, or that leaves no room for the kind of reflection I engage in concerning what might usefully be meant by the idea that a standard of conduct is 'rational' or 'objective'?. . . Is not an ethical theory that begins by configuring the field in Ron's way likely to truncate certain discussions before they are allowed to begin?"[16]

Although Stout disagreed with Barney Twiss' interpretation of his position, he was more charitable towards him. As he turned his attention from Green to Twiss, he said: "Instead of defining me out of the profession, ignoring most of my arguments, and treating the rest carelessly, Barney accords them the respect of close reading and charitable reconstruction."[17] Twiss had suggested that in contrast to the correspondence theory of truth supported by many ethicists, the key to Stout's position is a coherence view of truth. "This coherentist approach to moral justification requires not only the rejection of foundational beliefs but also the rejection of the idea of a universal practical reason that might somehow ground those beliefs."[18] Stout's response to this aspect of Twiss' critique helps to clarify my own reaction to readers of an earlier version of this study who expressed disappointment that I did not say more about the foundational beliefs underlying my position. One reader claimed that I did not go far enough in my attempt to illumine the relationship between basic convictions and concrete judgments about the pipeline, while another suggested that I had failed to explain why my stance regarding moral issues such as the pipeline proposal was finally nothing more than a subjective preference. I had appeared to reject foundationalism without making it clear what I was putting in its place.

Like Stout, I believe that "The issues worth taking a stand on are often one or two levels closer to earth than the levels on which the philosophical isms operate."[19] Whereas Green, Twiss and other foundationalists focus attention on the theory used to justify and ground the truth claims and moral judgments that are made in concrete everyday situations, Stout concentrates on the truth claims and moral judgments themselves and on how they emerge in the give and take of a policy debate. Referring to the work of a sceptical realist to whom Twiss compares his position, Stout says "You can have the concept of moral truth and an ethos of fallibility and self-criticism without settling the highfalutin philosophical debates."[20]

On the one hand, the pragmatic, historicist, holist (to use terms Stout appears to accept regarding his position) ethicist proceeds with the reconstruction of actual debates without assuming that basic philosophical issues about the ultimate status of truth claims and moral judgments need to be resolved either by or on behalf of participants in the debate in order to have serious moral discourse. This does not mean that it is never appropriate to discuss, and even to debate, such foundational issues. The point, rather, for the pragmatist is that resolving such issues is not a precondition for continuing the debate.

On the other hand, Stout is making a stronger claim about the limitations of what I referred to above as hard foundationalism. Insofar as foundationalists give the impression that fundamental principles function in a deductive, context-free manner, we are being seriously misled about the nature of morality.[21] The imperious demand to be rational can undermine our attempts to be reasonable. We can make our differing positions intelligible to one another without having to assume that they have thus become rationally binding on the other.[22]

There are haunting echoes of the context vs. principles debate of the 1960s, and of the current debate in Roman Catholic circles between traditionalists and proportionalists in what I have been saying. Just as James Gustafson argued in the sixties that this was a misplaced debate, we should be wary of the way in which present relations between foundationalists and pragmatists have become polarized. It should be possible to extend the range of the comparative ethics discipline to encompass diversity in basic orientations so that foundationalists and pragmatists need not simply read one another out of the profession. Evidence that Ronald Green shares this goal is provided by an article he coauthored in 1986 with Charles Reynolds. They call for a more comprehensive approach to comparative studies and for a move from "thin" to "thick" theories as the guiding direction for the discipline.[23]

In this study of the pipeline debate I have focused primarily on the debate itself without assuming that I have resolved the philosophical debates going on within the discipline. I have attempted to employ a framework for description and analysis which is sufficiently comprehensive to incorporate philosophical and theological concerns with foundational issues, even though my own interests and training bring me closer to Stout's pragmatic, historical approach than to Green's more abstract, foundationalist approach. Rather than thinking in terms of mutually exclusive options, I find it more useful to focus attention on different levels of discourse which accomplish different functions in a comprehensive approach to comparative ethics. I will return to this point after I have introduced the other source of tension within the discipline.

The second type of tension in relation to which I will attempt to locate this study is between "engagement" and "detachment" on the part of the ethicist. In his paper to the Religious Social Ethics Group of the American Academy of Religion in October 1974, Ralph Potter called for a more sharply focused discipline of social ethics and for greater scholarly detachment on the part of ethicists as ethicists.[24] Responses generated by Potter's paper suggest that he touched upon a very live issue. In his response to Potter's emphasis on the reflective task and consultative role of the ethicist, Joseph Hough claimed that "the task of Christian social ethics is to advocate particular ethical positions on the basis of Christian ethical criteria." He felt Potter's emphasis on the passive role of the ethicist would play into the hands of "current conservative trends in the culture and in the churches."[25]

My description of comparative ethics, and the fact that I did not become more active as a participant in Project North's activities, create the impression that I must be closer to Potter's emphasis on the limitations of the ethicist's task than to the vanguardist role Hough recommends for social ethicists. Such a conclusion needs to be qualified for at least two reasons. First, my differences with Hough are more situational than methodological. Hough was reflecting upon his own involvement in a program to fight racism in an increasingly conservative church and society in the United States during the Reagan years. My study is about the prophetic activity of Project North, which was officially sponsored and financed by the mainline Canadian churches during a slightly later period. As an academic I am neither above the battle looking down nor out in front trying to drag a conservative church forward.

As an ethicist, I have a role to play in the conversation through which church activists, other church leaders and members and church-related academics together assess the faithfulness and effectiveness of particular activities. Looking back upon those activities to see how the issues were perceived, how judgments were made and defended, and how different groups within the churches related to one another is an integral part of the action-reflection process of the churches themselves. Just as the surgeon adopts a specialized focus and disciplined detachment to diagnose and remove a tumour, the ethicist applies her or his specialized training to diagnose and to cure distorted communication. In neither case does specialization and detachment reflect a lack of commitment to the remedy being sought.

The second reason for qualifying the judgment that my approach to comparative ethics sounds more like Potter's passive, consultative style than Hough's advocacy model is that, as with most studies, this analysis of the pipeline debate moves back and forth along the engaged-detached axis. From the standpoint of whether or not the pipeline ought to be built, I help to rationalize (i.e., to clarify the ethical and theological reasons for) the churches' controversial anti-pipeline stand. Proponents of the pipeline will therefore see me as an engaged and biased critic of the pipeline. On the other hand, my willingness to provide a sympathetic account of the critics of Project North's confrontational style will make me appear at best detached and at worst unsympathetic to the liberationist cause.[26]

During the pipeline debate the prophetic arm of the churches both contributed to and frustrated the goals of open, undistorted communication and an inclusive conversation. By pressing the moral and religious aspects of the debate the churches, acting through the inter-church coalition Project North, helped to expand the framework within which the debate took place. However, the way in which Project North drew sharp lines between the converted and the unconverted, and between prisoners of greed and opponents of injustice, reflected a tendency to deal with opponents as stereotypes rather than as moral agents and participants in a serious public debate.[27]

One of the lessons to be drawn from this study of the pipeline debate is that it is possible to be in solidarity with particular participants in the debate and to keep one's position open to the scrutiny of persons with different commitments, orientations and basic premises. The methodological key to this both-and stance regarding the foundationalist-pragmatic and detached-engaged polarities is the identification of different levels of discourse. This aspect of my approach to the discipline of ethics owes a great deal to the influence of Gibson Winter and James Gustafson.

The publication of Gibson Winter's *Elements for a Social Ethic* in 1966 was a major event, especially for his students who had been trying to decipher the meaning of the new direction in which his thought seemed to be going.[28] As one of those students, my initial response to Winter's claim that neo-orthodox theology had not provided an adequate foundation for social ethics was that he had abandoned theology altogether. When I returned to Canada for doctoral studies I discovered obvious affinities between Winter's approach in *Elements* and the works of United Church scholars such as Gregory Vlastos, R.B.Y. Scott, Martyn Estall, John Line and other members of the Fellowship for a Christian Social Order.[29] In ways that Alasdair MacIntyre has helped me to understand, *Elements for a Social Ethic* helped me to become re-rooted in my liberal Protestant United Church tradition. It is in relation to that tradition that I finally deal with the foundational and pragmatic aspects of the ethicist's tasks and the detached and engaged dimensions of the ethicist's identity.[30]

In *Elements*, Winter used a phenomenological approach to distinguish among common sense, scientific and ideological perspectives on the everyday world; to clarify the relationships among different styles of social science; and to clarify the relationship between science and ethics. The distinctions used in this study between story-telling and analysis, and within analysis between factual and ethical levels of clarification presuppose Winter's work in *Elements*. My analysis in Chapter 4 of the debate over the likely impact of the proposed pipeline on native communities draws heavily on Winter's discussion of the relationships among different styles of social science and between social science and social ethics.

During the late 1970s and early 1980s Winter and I collaborated on a paper for the American Association for the Advancement of Science.[31] On the basis of that paper on the role of citizens and experts in public policy debates we were invited to participate in a World Council of Churches' consultation on political ethics. That experience increased my awareness of the role of story-telling as an integral part of ethical and theological reflection. It also reaffirmed for me the importance of a self-consciously developed comparative approach to the task of moving from story-telling to analysis.[32]

In his 1981 book, *Liberating Creation: Foundations of Religious Social Ethics*, Winter used material from my study of the Mackenzie Valley pipeline debate as the basis for exploring the metaphors and symbols embedded in different perceptions of and visions for the North. I will return to this study in Chapter 6 when I deal explicitly with the role of religious convictions in debates about public policies. However, my tendency to stress the pragmatic rather than the foundational dimensions of the debate means that it is *Elements* rather than *Liberating Creation* which has had the greatest impact on my approach in this study.

Gustafson has influenced my understanding of Protestant social ethics both as an interpreter of H. Richard Niebuhr and through his persistent refusal to choose between situational and principled approaches to the discipline. The most direct source of the levels of clarification which I will describe in the next chapter was his article, "Context vs. Principles: A Misplaced Debate." In the conclusion I will return to his dogged defence of casuistry when that approach to practical moral reasoning had fallen out of favour even with Roman Catholic moral theologians, and to his identification of different modes of discourse in recent church and society documents of the World Council of Churches.

As further background for my analysis of the numerous conversations that together made up the Mackenzie Valley pipeline debate, I will now say a few words about the debate itself.

2. The Mackenzie Valley Pipeline Debate

The discovery of oil and natural gas at Prudhoe Bay, Alaska, in 1968 drew Canadian attention to the possibility that oil and gas could be found in the Canadian North in sufficient quantities to justify development if they could be shipped south in pipelines carrying Alaskan oil and gas to US markets in the south. When more oil than gas was found in Prudhoe Bay, the Americans decided to build an oil pipeline across Alaska and to ship the oil by tanker down the coast.

Although it would be possible to handle Alaskan natural gas in the same fashion, the need to liquefy it in order to transport it by tanker increased the attractiveness of an overland route across Canada. In March 1974 Canadian Arctic Gas Pipelines Limited (also called Arctic Gas), a consortium of twenty-seven companies, applied to the Government of Canada for permission to build a pipeline to carry natural gas from Alaska and the Canadian North to markets in southern Canada and the United States (Figure 1, p. 12).

In the summer of 1974 Mr. Justice Thomas R. Berger was appointed to inquire into the impact of pipeline construction on native communities and on the fragile northern environment and to specify the terms and conditions which would have to be met if such a pipeline was built. After extensive formal hearings involving the testimony and cross-examination of expert witnesses and less formal hearings in the thirty-five communities of the Mackenzie Valley and in ten southern cities, Berger recommended in May 1977 that no pipeline be constructed along the Mackenzie Valley for at least ten years. The National Energy Board, which also held extensive hearings, arrived at the same conclusion.[33]

By the time the Berger Inquiry was under way a second applicant had entered the competition for permission to build a northern pipeline. First, Foothills Pipelines Limited proposed building a pipeline which would follow an all-Canadian route along the Mackenzie Valley (Figure 2, p. 13). This proposal was later abandoned in favour of the ultimately successful bid to build a pipeline along the Alaska Highway (Figure 3, p. 14). This line would carry Alaskan gas to southern markets in the United States with the possibility of a connecting link to Canadian reserves in the Mackenzie Delta and the Beaufort Sea along the Dempster Highway. In the fall of 1977, Canadian and United States governments signed an agreement to proceed with the Alaska Highway pipeline. Plans were soon in place to pre-build the southern section so that revenue generated by natural gas exports from Alberta could be used to finance the northern line. The northern section of the Alaska Highway pipeline has not been completed, but there is renewed interest in the shorter route along the Mackenzie Valley.[34]

In the summer of 1977 when Berger and the National Energy Board announced their negative conclusions regarding both the Canadian Arctic Gas Pipeline Limited (Arctic Gas) and the Foothills Pipe Lines Limited proposals for a Mackenzie Valley pipeline, only the pipeline applicants seemed very surprised. Not enough gas had been discovered and a pipeline no longer seemed economically feasible. However, when Arctic Gas filed its application in 1974, construction of a Mackenzie Valley pipeline looked inevitable, and it was assumed to be in the public interest. At that time not much attention was paid to the question of whether or not the pipeline ought to be built. A number of factors converged to shatter the aura of inevitability that initially surrounded the proposal. A major factor was the emergence on the scene of an alternative proposal. Each side's experts undermined the credibility of the other side's technical submissions, thereby giving unexpected support to critics who questioned the feasibility of both proposals.

Another factor was the strong support by public interest groups such as the churches for the northern native peoples' call for a moratorium on pipeline construction until their land claims had been settled. My interest in the role of the churches does not imply that I believe that they necessarily played a decisive role in transforming the pipeline proposal from an inevitable next step into a public debate. Although the churches were not the major actors determining the final outcome of the debate, they did play an important role. As critics of the pipeline proposal the churches, along with the native peoples and other public interest groups, helped to push the debate beyond narrowly technical and economic considerations. They also provided the organizational skills and financial resources required to enable hundreds of Canadians to learn at first hand how the native peoples saw the issue and why they felt that justice demanded a moratorium until their claims had been settled.

3. Project North

During the 1960s a renewed commitment to social justice on the part of the Canadian churches was given added energy by a new level of ecumenical co-operation. In 1965 ten churches and ten other voluntary organizations sponsored a conference on health care. It was timed to coincide with the release of Emmett Hall's report of the Royal Commission on Health Services. Firm support was given to the report's main recommendation that Canadians should have a universally accessible, publicly funded health care system. By the late 1960s poverty had once again become a front-burner issue. In May 1968 twelve churches plus the federal government and several provincial governments co-sponsored a major conference on "The Christian Conscience and Poverty." The key ideas of the day were development and participation. The resources and technological capacities of the world, and particularly of wealthy countries like Canada, should be directed towards the provision of basic human needs and aspirations. In addition to security from the fear of sickness and poverty, all people had a right to participate in the decisions affecting their lives.

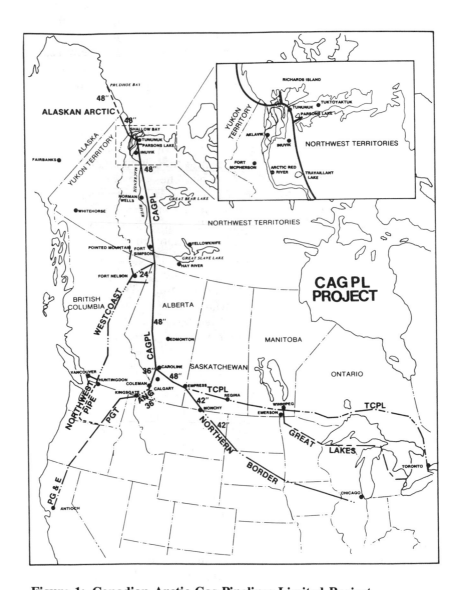

Figure 1: Canadian Arctic Gas Pipelines Limited Project
Source: National Energy Board, *Reasons for Decision: Northern Pipelines*, vol. 1
(Ottawa: Supply and Services Canada, 1977), Map 3-3.

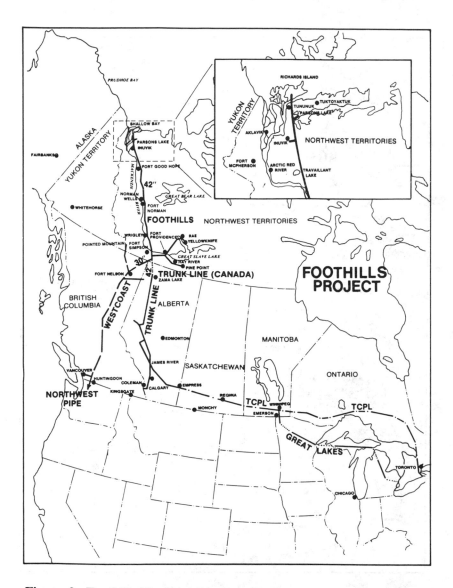

Figure 2: Foothills Pipelines Limited Project—Mackenzie Valley
Source: National Energy Board, *Reasons for Decision: Northern Pipelines*, vol. 1
(Ottawa: Supply and Services Canada, 1977), Map 3-3.

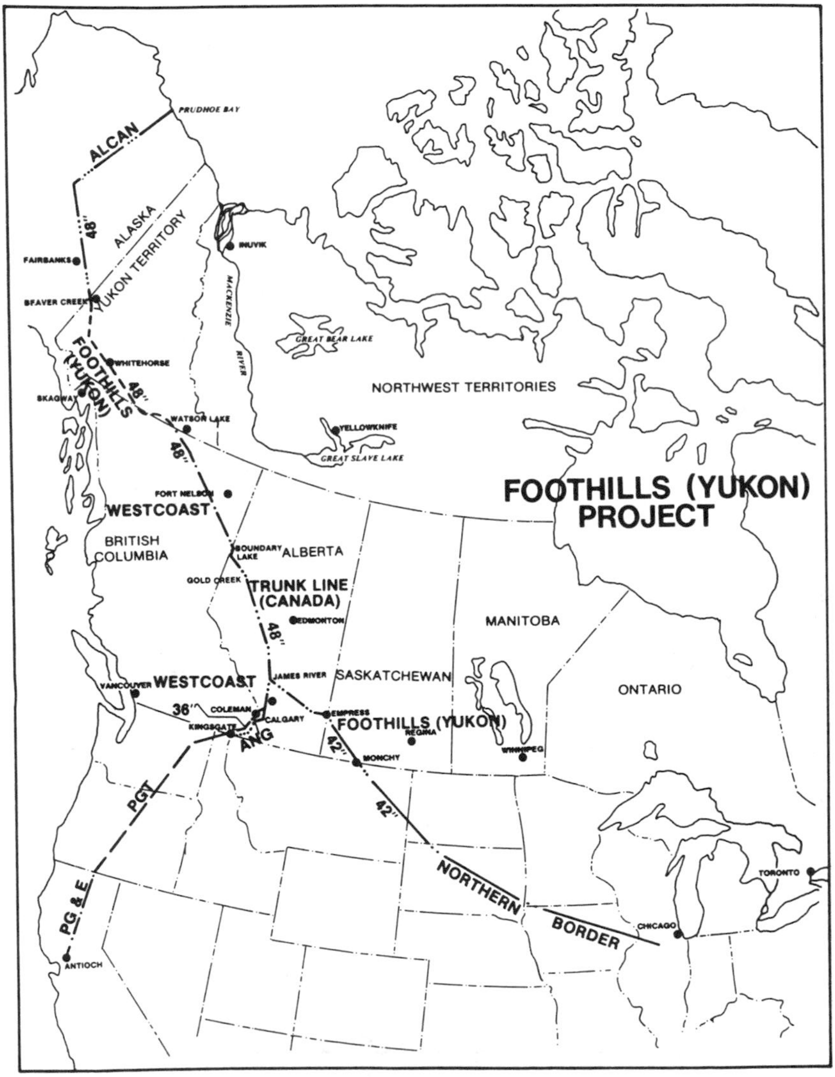

Figure 3: Foothills Pipelines Limited Project—Alaska Highway
Source: National Energy Board, *Reasons for Decision: Northern Pipelines*, vol. 1
(Ottawa: Supply and Services Canada, 1977), Map 3-8.

It is not surprising that such thoughts led the churches to radical reassessments of their relations with native peoples. During an earlier period they had played crucial roles in the process through which Canada's original citizens had been both impoverished and reduced to the status of wards of a paternalistic government. By the 1960s the churches added their voices to the call for renewed dialogue about the administration of native affairs. When the Trudeau government released its 1969 white paper on Indian Policy which presupposed the complete assimilation of natives into the dominant Canadian society, the churches supported native leaders who argued that they wanted participation but not assimilation.[35]

There were two major obstacles in the way of full participation by native peoples in Canadian public life. First, it was not widely believed, particularly by government and industry leaders, that native Canadians ought to be treated as distinct peoples with a right to self-determination.[36] Second, massive resource development schemes were already in the planning if not construction stages before particular native communities were consulted or involved in a decision-making process. By 1975 the Anglican, Roman Catholic and United Churches had official policies which declared that the native peoples' right to participate as equals had priority over any development projects being planned for lands which had not been given up through treaties. They were thus ready to translate these resolutions into effective solidarity actions when they received a proposal to fund an experimental two-year project to help northern native organizations to communicate their concerns to southern Canadians.

In the spring and summer of 1975 Karmel McCullum and Hugh McCullum travelled across the North doing research for their book, *This Land Is Not For Sale*.[37] By the time they had completed the book they were alarmed by the threat so many native communities were experiencing from proposed mega-projects. Native organizations were becoming stronger, but they could see an important role for the churches as communication links between northern natives and southern Canadians. The Anglican and United churches and the Roman Catholic bishops agreed to contribute $8500 per year each for a two-year project which would begin on September 1, 1975. Thus Project North joined other coalitions such as the Taskforce on the Churches and Corporate Responsibility, GATT-Fly, Ten Days for World Development, the Inter-Church Project on Population, and the Inter-Church Committee on Chile (later the Inter-Church Committee on Human Rights in Latin America) as one of the new experiments in Canadian ecumenism.[38]

The Project North staff team and the Administrative Committee made up of representatives from the sponsoring denominations worked with a large number of native organizations on a wide range of concerns. During the Berger years, however, they were particularly closely involved with the Indian Brotherhood of the Northwest Territories (Dene Nation).[39] Since my focus is on the Berger Inquiry and the Mackenzie Valley pipeline debate, it is that aspect of Project North's work that will receive the most attention. I hope that this study of one aspect of Project North's activities will stimulate someone else to tell the full story.[40]

As long as no final decision had been made regarding the Mackenzie Valley, Alaska Highway, Polar Gas or Norman Wells pipelines, Project North campaigned tirelessly against these pipelines in solidarity with native peoples such as the Dene and Métis of the Mackenzie Valley, the Inuvialuit of the Western Arctic and the Council of Yukon Indians. Over fifty local groups were formed across the country in support of the moratorium and native rights. During the decade following the Mackenzie Valley pipeline debate attention shifted first to the battle against Bill C-48, the Canada Oil and Gas Lands legislation asserting federal control over northern resources, and then to the struggle to have the native rights clause reinstated in the Constitution. There was also continuing support for the Nishga Indians of British Columbia, particularly in their attempt to stop Amax from dumping mine tailings in their fishing grounds. Other solidarity activities included support for the Lubicon Lake Band of Alberta, and the Innu of Labrador.[41]

By the end of the 1980s, the sponsoring churches decided that there was a need for a fresh start in their aboriginal rights work, and a new covenant among the churches, local Project North groups and native peoples. In 1989 the Inter-Church Aboriginal Rights Coalition (Project North) was created, with its office in Ottawa. The churches hope that organizational changes will represent a creative response to new realities, and that the vision which inspired the churches to create Project North in 1975 will live on through the new coalition.[42]

Notes

1. Ronald M. Green and Charles H. Reynolds, "Cosmology and the 'Question of Ethics,' " *Journal of Religious Ethics*, 14, 1 (Spring 1986): 143.

2. See "Focus on Theravada Buddhist Ethics," *Journal of Religious Ethics*, 7, 1 (Spring 1979): 1-64; and "Focus on Comparative Religious Ethics," *Journal of Religious Ethics*, 9, 1 (Fall 1981): 157-227. For an illustration of the tendency to assume that Christian studies are not part of comparative ethics, see the cumulative index of articles in the Fall 1987 issue of the *Journal of Religious Ethics*. The Spring 1985 issue had featured a three-article focus on the ethics of taxation. The subsection of the index devoted to comparative ethics included the

Islamic perspective on taxation, but it did not include the articles dealing with Roman Catholic and Protestant teachings about taxation.

3. See David Little and Sumner B. Twiss, *Comparative Religious Ethics: A New Method* (San Francisco: Harper & Row, 1978); Ronald M. Green, *Religious Reason* (New York: Oxford University Press, 1978); and *Religion and Moral Reason: A New Method for Comparative Study* (New York and Oxford: Oxford University Press, 1988); and Fred Bird, "Paradigms and Parameters for the Comparative Study of Religious and Ideological Ethics," *Journal of Religious Ethics*, 9, 2 (Fall 1981): 157-85.

4. Jeffrey Stout, *The Flight from Authority: Religion, Morality, and the Quest for Autonomy* (Notre Dame and London: University of Notre Dame Press, 1981); and *Ethics After Babel: The Languages of Morals and Their Discontents* (Boston: Beacon Press, 1988).

5. Roger Hutchinson, "Towards 'A Pedagogy for Allies of the Oppressed,' " *Studies in Religion/Sciences Religieuses*, 13, 2 (1984): 145-50.

6. Roger Hutchinson, "Comparative Ethics and the MacKenzie Valley Pipeline Debate," *Toronto Journal of Theology*, 1, 2 (Fall 1985): 242-60.

7. Although this way of formulating the problem has a distinctly Lonergonian ring to it, my own introduction to this type of thinking (or to thinking in relation to ideal types) took place at Queen's Theological College while studying H. Richard Niebuhr with Donald Mathers and at the Divinity School of the University of Chicago where Gibson Winter and Alvin Pitcher helped me to overcome my distrust of typologies. See Alvin Pitcher and Gibson Winter, "Perspectives in Religious Social Ethics," *Journal of Religious Ethics*, 5, 1 (Spring 1977): 69-90; Bernard Lonergan, *Method in Theology* (New York: Herder and Herder, 1982; and Bernard Lonergan, "The Example of Gibson Winter," in *A Second Collection: Papers* by Bernard J.F. Lonergan, S.J., ed. Wm.F.J. Ryan, S.J., and Bernard J. Tyrrell, S.J. (London: Darton, Longman & Todd, 1974), pp. 189-192.

8. For a comment on the methodological discussions of the Religious Social Ethics Group, see Glen H. Stassen, "Editorial Notes," *Journal of Religious Ethics*, 5, 1 (Spring 1977): 1-8.

9. Alasdair MacIntyre, *Whose Justice? Which Rationality?* (Notre Dame, Indiana: University of Notre Dame Press, 1988), p. 6.

10. Ibid., p. 6.

11. Ibid., p. 6.

12. Deductive reasoning draws logical conclusions by going from the general to the particular. This type of reasoning can be illustrated by the well-known syllogism: All men are mortal. Socrates is a man. Therefore, Socrates is mortal. Inductive reasoning, on the other hand, moves from particular instances towards general laws. For example, we learn from experience that more happiness results when we are kind to one another.

13. Little and Twiss had attempted to develop a middle way between an "apples and oranges" approach, which stresses cultural differences and casts doubt upon the possibility of non-imperialistic comparative studies, and "grand theory" approaches, which reduce the richness of particular traditions to fit the concepts of a particular grand theory. In response to Green's criticism for not looking harder for the deep structure of religious thought embedded in all traditions, Little explained the inadequacies of Green's grand theory. Stout, on the other hand, accused Little and Twiss of escaping the Kantian rationalism of Green's grand theory by retreating into the reductionist definitions and concepts of the

logical positivists. Little's response to Stout was that his form of holism simply represented a version of the "apples and oranges" approach which made comparative studies impossible. See David Little, "The Present State of the Comparative Study of Religious Ethics," *Journal of Religious Ethics*, 9, 2 (Fall 1981): 210-27; Ronald Green, "Review of Little and Twiss, *Comparative Religious Ethics*," *Journal of Religion*, 61, 1 (January 1981): 111-13; and Jeffrey Stout, "Holism and Comparative Ethics: A Response to Little," *Journal of Religious Ethics*, 11, 2 (Fall 1983): 301-16.

14.   See Ronald Green, "Jeffrey Stout's 'Ethics after Babel': A Critical Appraisal'"; Sumner B. Twiss, "On Truth and Justification in 'Ethics after Babel' "; and Jeffrey Stout, "Ism-Mongering: A Response to Green and Twiss," in *The Annual of the Society of Christian Ethics 1990* (Knoxville, Tennessee: Society of Christian Ethics, 1990), pp. 27-36, 37-53 and 54-62.

15.   Green, "Stout's 'Ethics after Babel,' " p. 29.

16.   Stout, "Ism-Mongering," p. 57.

17.   Ibid., p. 58.

18.   Twiss, "On Truth and Justification," p. 43.

19.   Stout, "Ism-Mongering," p. 61.

20.   Ibid., p. 61.

21.   See Jeffrey Stout, "Holism and Comparative Ethics: A Response to Little," *Journal of Religious Ethics,* 11, 2 (Fall 1983): 304. In response to Little's tendency to be encouraged by the fact that Stout had expressed appreciation for the value of one of the actual case studies in *Comparative Religious Ethics*, Stout pointed out that he had argued specifically "that some of the most salient virtues of the best chapter, the study of Matthew, had nothing to do with the method and could not plausibly be claimed as evidence for its vindication. The proof of the pudding may be in the eating, but the test of a recipe is rather more complicated than that. A cook who intuitively does more than his recipe demands may produce edible food, but he does not put his recipe to the test. The crucial question here, if I may extend the culinary metaphor a bit further, is not even whether the recipe, if rigorously followed, would produce edible food, but rather whether such food as that would be sufficiently rich and well balanced for a steady diet."

22.   For the distinction between reasonable and rational, see Northrop Frye, *The Double Vision: Language and Meaning in Religion* (Toronto: The United Church Publishing House, 1991), pp. 66-67: "The funeral service speaks of Christianity as providing the comfort of a reasonable religion. It is not always understood that the reasonable and the rational are opposed attitudes, and that the comfort of a reasonable religion can hardly coexist with the prickly discomfort of a rational one. The reasonable person proceeds by compromise, halfway measures, illogical agreements, and similar signs of mature human intelligence. Rationalism is a militant use of language designed to demonstrate the exclusive truth of what it works on and with."

23.   Green and Reynolds, "Cosmogony and the 'Question of Ethics,' " p. 143: "Having argued that Little and Twiss' proposal for work in religious ethics constitutes a point of departure for this field, we must now observe that it addresses only a fraction of the questions appropriate to a full theory of comparative religious ethics. Indeed, we might term theirs a 'thin' theory of ethics to contrast it with the 'thick' theory to which work in this area aspires."

24.   Ralph B. Potter, "The Logic of Moral Argument," in *Toward a Discipline of Social Ethics*, ed. Paul Deats (Boston: Boston University Press, 1972), pp. 93-114. For a summary of the discussion, see Stassen, "Editorial Notes," pp. 1-8.

25. Joseph C. Hough, Jr., "Christian Social Ethics as Advocacy," *Journal of Religious Ethics*, 5, 1 (Spring 1977): 115-16.

26. See Cranford Pratt and Roger Hutchinson, eds., *Christian Faith and Economic Justice: Toward a Canadian Perspective* (Burlington, Ont.: Trinity Press, 1988), especially Pratt's Chapter 10, "Faith and Social Action," pp. 161-77; and my Chapter 11, "Study and Action in Politically Divided Churches," pp. 178-92. For vigorous critiques of our approach in this book, see the articles by Lee Cormie, Travis Kroeker and Janet Silman in the *Toronto Journal of Theology*, 7, 1 (Spring 1991): 19-50.

27. My emphasis on conversation or interpersonal communication as a model for ethics and theology reflects various influences. The most important influence was Gibson Winter. See, in particular, *Elements for a Social Ethic* (New York: Macmillan, 1966); *Liberating Creation: Foundations of Religious Social Ethics* (New York: Crossroad, 1981); and our jointly authored chapter, "Towards a Method in Political Ethics," in *Perspectives on Political Ethics: An Ecumenical Inquiry*, ed. Kosan Srisang (Geneva: WCC Publications; and Washington, D.C.: Georgetown University Press, 1983), pp. 163-73. *Liberating Creation* draws on material from our paper "Citizens, Experts and Public Policy" presented at the 1981 meetings of the American Association for the Advancement of Science. The chapter in *Perspectives on Political Ethics* is a revised version of the methodological section of our paper "Political Ethics and the MacKenzie Valley Pipeline Inquiry" prepared for a World Council of Churches Consultation on Political Ethics in Cyprus in October 1981. See also my contribution to a *festschrift* for Winter, "Mutuality: Procedural Norm and Foundational Symbol," in *Liberation and Ethics: Essays in Religious Social Ethics in Honor of Gibson Winter*, ed. Charles Amjad-Ali and W. Alvin Pitcher (Chicago: Center for the Scientific Study of Religion, 1985), pp. 97-110. See also Charles Taylor's proposal for a "dialogue society," in *The Pattern of Politics* (Toronto/Montreal: McClelland and Stewart, 1970): 123-27.

28. Gibson Winter, *Elements for a Social Ethic*.

29. See my doctoral dissertation, "The Fellowship for a Christian Social Order: A Social Ethical Analysis of a Christian Socialist Movement" (Th.D. Dissertation, Toronto School of Theology, 1975); and Gregory Vlastos and R.B.Y. Scott, eds., *Towards the Christian Revolution* (Chicago: Willet and Clark, 1936; Kingston, Ont.: Ronald Frye, 1989).

30. MacIntyre, *Whose Justice? Which Rationality?* p. 7. MacIntyre suggests that there is an alternative mode of understanding which is better than unsupportable claims to universality, on the one hand, and the belief that truth claims are confined to particular communities of conviction, on the other. What we need to recover, according to MacIntyre, is "a conception of rational inquiry as embodied in a tradition, a conception according to which the standards of rational justification themselves emerge from and are part of the history in which they are vindicated by the way in which they transcend the limitations of and provide remedies for the defects of their predecessors within the history of that same tradition."

31. Gibson Winter and Roger Hutchinson, "Citizens, Experts and Public Policy: Canadian Churches and the Mackenzie Valley Pipeline Inquiry," The American Association for the Advancement of Science, Toronto, Ontario, 6 January 1980 (unpublished typescript).

32. Roger Hutchinson, "Cyprus Consultation on Political Ethics," *The Ecumenist*, 20, 2 (January-February 1982): 27-29.

33. The most readable account of the pipeline debate and the reasons for Berger's conclusions remains the Commissioner's own report: Mr. Justice Thomas R. Berger, *Northern Frontier, Northern Homeland: The Report of the MacKenzie Valley Pipeline Inquiry*, vol. 1 (Ottawa: Ministry of Supply and Services Canada, 1977). See also, Robert Page, *Northern Development and the Canadian Dilemma* (Toronto: McClelland and Stewart, 1986); and François Bregha, *Bob Blair's Pipeline: The Business and Politics of Northern Energy Development Projects* (Toronto: James Lorimer, 1979; rev. ed., 1982).

34. François Bregha, "The Mackenzie Valley Pipeline Revisited," *Probe Post* (Spring 1989): 30-31. See also, Drew Fagan, "NWT Supports Proposal for Huge Exports of Gas"; and "Foothills Seeks NEB Nod for MacKenzie Pipeline," *The Globe and Mail*, Toronto edition, 15 March 1989, pp. B1-B2; and 17 March 1989, pp. B1-B2. Northwest Territories Energy Minister Nellie Cournoyer was an active opponent of the pipeline proposal in 1977. She now supports it because the Inuvialuit of the Western Arctic have obtained a land claim settlement which will allow them to benefit from development, and there are agreements in principle between the federal government and the Dene and Métis of the Mackenzie Valley.

35. Charles Hendry had been asked in 1967 to undertake a major study of the relationship between the Anglican Church and native peoples. See his very important report, *Beyond Traplines* (Toronto: Anglican Book Centre, 1969).

36. See Roger Hutchinson, "Native Peoples in a Technological Society: The Struggle for Self-Determination," presented at the XIVth Congress of the International Association of the History of Religions, Winnipeg, Manitoba, 17-22 August 1980; and Patrick Kerans, "The Struggle Against Dependency: Equality as Individuals or as Peoples," in *Traditions in Contact and Change*, ed. Peter Slater, Don Wiebe, Maurice Boutin and Harold Coward (Waterloo, ON: Wilfrid Laurier University Press, 1983).

37. Hugh and Karmel McCullum, *This Land Is Not For Sale: Canada's Original People and Their Land, A Saga of Neglect, Exploitation, and Conflict* (Toronto: Anglican Book Centre, 1975).

38. See the Canadian Council of Churches' *Directory 1988-Annuaire 1988* (a directory of national interchurch social action coalitions and other groups); and Roger Hutchinson, "Ecumenical Witness in Canada: Social Action Coalitions," *International Review of Mission*, 71 (1982): 344-53. During 1976 the Lutheran Church in America (Canada Section), the Presbyterian Church in Canada and the Mennonite Central Committee (Canada) became participants in Project North. Later, additional sponsors included the Society of Jesus, the Oblate Conference in Canada, the Religious Society of Friends and the Christian Reformed Churches in Canada.

39. Roger Hutchinson, "The Dene and Project North: Partners in Mission," in *Religion/Culture: Comparative Canadian Studies, Canadian Issues*, 7, ed. William Westfall, Louis Rousseau, Fernand Harvey and John Simpson (Ottawa: Association for Canadian Studies, 1985): 391-410.

40. The Project North Archives are in the General Synod Archives of the Anglican Church of Canada. Additional research materials are housed at the Centre for the Study of Religion in Canada at Emmanuel College, University of Toronto.

41. Good summaries of Project North's work have been provided by the chairpersons of the Administrative Committee in the *Project North Journal*, 11, 4 (Winter 1987): Tony Clarke (Roman Catholic, September 1975-April 1981), "The Cry for Justice: A Creative Response," pp. 1-4; Clifton L. Monk (Lutheran, April 1981-September 1983), "Spirited Actions of Conviction," pp. 5-7; Menno Wiebe

(Mennonite, September 1983-May 1986), "Writing Canada's History: The Next Chapter," pp. 8-10; and Peter Hamel (Anglican, May 1986-September 1987), "Partnerships Multiply Actions," pp. 11-13.

42. For this interpretation of the transition to a new organization, see Peter Hamel, "Redeeming the Vision: A New Covenant," *Project North Journal*, 11, 4 (Winter 1987) 14-16. For a less optimistic account, see Mike Milne, "Project North: The Death of a Vision," *United Church Observer* (October 1987): 9-12.

Chapter 1

A Mackenzie Valley Pipeline:
From Inevitable Next Step to Public Debate

"We are now at our last frontier. . . . Profound issues, touching our deepest concerns as a nation, await us there." When Mr. Justice Thomas Berger made this comment in 1977 he had just completed one of the most highly publicized inquiries in Canadian history. He has been both praised and criticized for his conclusion that it was time to ask not only how to build a northern pipeline but whether one should be built. This challenge was given added force by Berger's reminder that the North was not simply southern Canada's frontier. It is "the homeland of the Dene, Inuit and Métis, as it is also the home of the white people who live there." The North is also a unique environmental heritage. The Mackenzie Valley Pipeline Inquiry was, therefore, not simply about a northern pipeline. It was "about the protection of the northern environment and the future of northern peoples."[1]

The Mackenzie Valley pipeline debate was also about the way of life and priorities of southern Canadians. Our presumed energy needs provided the main justification for the pipeline, and our dominant assumptions about progress and development made such a project appear to be necessary, inevitable, and insofar as the question was even asked, morally responsible. Once the necessity and inevitability of the pipeline were no longer obvious, the ethical issues also came into clearer view. It is this aspect of the debate that is my primary concern in this study. In this chapter I will introduce the debate, explain my focus on the role of the churches, and identify the key elements of the method to be used for analysing the debate.

1. The Second Great Pipeline Debate

The Mackenzie Valley pipeline debate of the 1970s took place against the background of the great debate of the 1950s over the construction of the trans-Canada natural gas pipeline. That earlier debate is remembered primarily for the authoritarian tactics used by C.D. Howe and the Liberal government. Their use of closure to rush through the pipeline bill in time to meet the company's June 7, 1956, deadline had serious political consequences. It was a crucial factor in the Progressive Conservatives' slim victory in 1957 and landslide in 1958. The distinguishing feature of the Mackenzie Valley pipeline debate, on the other hand, was the new level of public participation which seemed to be achieved. What the two debates had in common was the way they touched many of the same issues that lie close to the heart of the Canadian identity.

William Kilbourn's comment about writing the history of Trans-Canada Pipelines applies with equal force to attempts to understand the debate over the proposed Mackenzie Valley pipeline and energy corridor:

> Any account of its long struggle to be born inevitably raises most of the classic issues in Canada's survival as a nation: American economic influence and the nature of Canadian-American relations; the debate between north-south continentalism and east-west nationalism; the questions of transportation and national unity, of energy and national growth, of control over natural resources and their exploitation; the latent conflict between western producer and eastern consumer; dominion-provincial relations; the problem of public versus private enterprise and the compromise of the crown corporation; the connections between business and politics, the role of the regulatory bodies between them; the rights of Parliament; and the place of popular feelings, pressure groups and the press in the difficult matter of making difficult decisions on complex issues of great national importance.[2]

Once the decision had been made to build a trans-Canada pipeline to link western gas to eastern markets it seemed unlikely that the expansion of this system would be controversial. For Trans-Canada Pipelines Limited, additional pipelines to tap northern supplies would simply be the inevitable next steps in the task of linking natural gas supplies to the densely populated areas of the continent. As Kilbourn observed in 1970:

> The essential challenge for the Company in the future . . . lay not in diversification, but in developing and expanding the role for which it was originally chartered—the moving of Canada's most important new energy supply from west to east across the centre of the continent. By 1970, Trans-Canada had only just begun to tap the immense reserves of the western provinces and the Arctic territories.[3]

As early as 1960, Trans-Canada had authorized feasibility studies "to consider ways of tapping the vast reserves of the Peace River district in northern Alberta and northwestern British Columbia and linking them up to markets around Chicago and Detroit."[4] In 1967 Trans-Canada, along with two American pipeline companies, initiated "a feasibility study of a natural gas pipeline from the Liard Basin in the southwestern region of the Northwest Territories."[5] Attention shifted farther north following the 1968 discovery of what promised to be the largest oil and gas field in North America at Prudhoe Bay. In July 1970 a twelve-million-dollar feasibility study of a pipeline to the American midwest was announced by the Northwest Project Study Group (a consortium consisting of Trans-Canada Pipelines, two American gas companies and three oil companies with gas reserves at Prudhoe Bay).[6]

Meanwhile, Alberta Gas Trunk Line Limited, after an unsuccessful attempt to join the Northwest Project Study Group, joined with Canadian National Railways and four US pipeline firms to create Canadian Gas Arctic Systems Study Group in June 1970. In 1972 the groups backed by Trans-Canada Pipelines and Alberta Gas Trunk Lines merged to form Canadian Arctic Gas Study Group Limited. By the time this group filed its application for clearances to build a Mackenzie Valley natural gas pipeline in March 1974 its name had been changed to Canadian Arctic Gas Pipelines Limited. I will usually refer to this applicant as Arctic Gas although occasionally, particularly in quotations, reference might be made to CAGPL.

Shortly after Arctic Gas filed its application, Alberta Gas Trunk Line Limited withdrew from the consortium and joined Westcoast Transmission Company Limited to create Foothills Pipelines Limited. In March 1975 Foothills applied for the necessary clearances to build an all-Canadian line from the Mackenzie Delta up the Mackenzie Valley to link with existing pipelines in northern British Columbia and Alberta. The application for this Maple Leaf line was later withdrawn in favour of the ultimately successful proposal to build a pipeline along the Alaska Highway to carry Alaskan gas to the lower forty-eight states.

Initial responses by the federal government to the discovery of oil and gas at Prudhoe Bay and in the Arctic Islands were not designed to encourage a full and open debate about a northern pipeline. The Task Force on Northern Oil Development, consisting of the deputy ministers of Energy Mines and Resources, Transport, Indian and Northern Affairs and the Chairman of the National Energy Board, was created in December 1968 to "formulate the government's response to the challenge posed by the development of the Alaskan reserves." As François Bregha points out, this high level committee very quickly "outgrew its original mandate to become a tireless advocate of Mackenzie Valley oil and gas pipelines."[7] Further support for a pipeline came in May 1970 when a meeting of top officials from relevant government departments declared that the construction of a Mackenzie Valley pipeline would be in the national interest.

Politicians also took it for granted that a northern pipeline would serve Canadian interests. In March 1971 Jean Chrétien, Minister of Indian Affairs and Northern Development, assured Dallas oilmen that "We in Canada would welcome the building of such a gas pipeline through our country and would do everything that is reasonable to facilitate this particular development."[8] In an April 1972 election campaign speech Prime Minister Trudeau announced plans for a Mackenzie Valley highway. The route would be carefully selected "so that it will be indispensable when oil and gas pipelines are built along the Mackenzie Valley." The road would be completed before pipeline companies began their projects "and will therefore offer considerable cost savings to them during the construction period."[9]

Appealing to what seemed at the time to be an inspiring historical precedent, Trudeau compared the proposed Mackenzie Valley transportation corridor to the "opening" of the West and the construction of the Canadian Pacific Railway:

> A transportation system is the key to national development in the North. This northern transportation system is mind-boggling in its size. But then so was the very concept of a continent-wide fur trade 100 years ago. It's expensive, but so was the Canadian Pacific Railway a century ago. Is it too big a project for Canada? Only in the view of those who have lost faith in what Canada is all about.[10]

In the 1972 election the Liberals were returned to power, but as a minority government. It became increasingly clear that for many Canadians the Canadian Pacific Railway was no longer celebrated as our "national dream." It was remembered as a symbol of metropolitan domination of the prairie hinterland. Even Anglophone Canadians had rediscovered Louis Riel as a hero of the Métis struggle for their prairie homeland. New questions were being asked about what Canada was all about. As Bregha suggests, the stage was set for a great debate over the next massive development project:

> By 1973 the Mackenzie pipeline had turned into a lightening rod for all those who were critical of the government's northern development policy. Public

interest groups such as Pollution Probe and the Canadian Arctic Resources Committee were increasingly effective in questioning the dubious assumptions under which the government was proceeding; economic nationalists led by the Committee for an Independent Canada articulated a latent public concern about the pace and purpose of resource exploitation in the Arctic; most importantly, the native people were now organized and united in their resistance to development prior to the settlement of their claims.[11]

When Arctic Gas applied for clearances to build a natural gas pipeline up the Mackenzie Valley in March 1974, the federal government decided that a full inquiry into its social, economic and environmental impact was required. Mr. Justice Thomas Berger of the British Columbia Supreme Court was appointed

> to inquire into and report upon the terms and conditions that should be imposed in respect of any right-of-way that might be granted across Crown lands for the purposes of the proposed Mackenzie Valley Pipeline having regard to (a) the social, environmental and economic impact regionally, of the construction, operation and subsequent abandonment of the proposed pipeline in the Yukon and Northwest Territories, and (b) any proposals to meet the specific environmental and social concerns set out in the Expanded Guidelines for Northern Pipelines.[12]

Berger held preliminary hearings in 1974 to clarify the scope and procedures of the Inquiry. Time was then given, and funding was provided, to allow the native peoples to prepare their responses to the pipeline applications. During 1975 and 1976 the Inquiry held formal hearings, which included the cross-examination of witnesses, and community hearings designed to let native peoples and other ordinary citizens speak in their own languages and in their own ways about the impact of a pipeline.

In the first volume of his report, tabled in the House of Commons on May 9, 1977, Berger recommended that for environmental reasons no pipeline should be permitted across the Northern Yukon. He also recommended that no pipeline should be built up the Mackenzie Valley until native claims had been settled and native peoples had time to develop institutions required to withstand the impact of a pipeline and to strengthen the traditional sector of their economy. He mentioned in passing that a pipeline along the Alaska Highway would probably be the least undesirable way to transport Alaskan gas to the southern US market. In July 1977 the National Energy Board reaffirmed Berger's conclusion, and on August 8, 1977, federal government approval of an Alaska Highway pipeline was announced.

The debate over the proposal to build a Mackenzie Valley pipeline has stimulated a great deal of discussion and analysis. Responses of scholars have not surprisingly reflected the interests and academic training of each scholar. This study is no exception. My teaching areas within the Toronto School of Theology and the University of Toronto's Centre for Religious Studies include church and society, Christian ethics and comparative ethics. My twofold interest, therefore, is in the role of the churches and in the ethical and ideological dimensions of the debate. These interests coincide insofar as the churches were active participants in the debate, and representatives of the churches and other religious organizations, such as the Committee for Justice and Liberty (now Citizens for Public Justice), insisted more persistently than most participants that moral and ideological issues should be part of the public debate.

My interests and training could have prompted me to focus on the encounter between northern natives, who were struggling to preserve or to recover a way of life threatened by industrial expansion, and southern whites, who took for granted the divine right of technologically advanced peoples to exploit frontier resources. That story was an important part of the pipeline debate, but it is not the central concern of this study.

In his review of Berger's report and the report of the Alaska Highway Pipeline Inquiry, Jim Lotz complained that both reports had failed to deal with "the most important question in the North today: the development of some sort of moral and ethical basis for action there." Clarifying this dimension of the debate will, according to Lotz, "require close scrutiny and understanding of the motives and assumptions of decision-makers in southern Canada." This will be difficult, because "Their territory is less well known, and more perilous, than the Canadian North has ever been."[13]

By intervening in the debate with strong demands regarding the rights of native peoples, the protection of the northern environment, and the need for all Canadians to shift from consumer to conserver values, leaders and members of the mainline Canadian churches entered the territory referred to by Lotz. They evoked reactions which provide a glimpse of the motives and assumptions of decision-makers in southern Canada. This study in comparative ethics represents a preliminary attempt to map that territory. The main comparison that interests me, therefore, is not the difference between native and white views of the land, attitudes towards technological progress, and so forth. The debate over the pipeline did not run neatly along native/non-native, north/south, Christian/non-Christian lines. It took place within these groups as well. My particular focus of attention in this study is on the debate between southern whites, and in particular within the churches. This way of focusing the study reflects my assumptions about the tasks of ethical reflection. On the one hand, the comparative ethicist seeks to identify and to understand what Fred Bird refers to as "moralities as cultural systems," that is, the shared systems of meaning or cultural systems within which moralities function as languages of persuasion.[14] On the other hand, it is the breakdown of taken-for-granted assumptions about what should be done and the fact of conflict within and between communities which provide the main occasions for ethical reflection. As Jon Gunnemann points out, as long as "moralities-in-place" remain unchallenged, there is little explicit awareness that moral issues are involved in the routine practices of daily life.[15] The pipeline debate both created tensions within the churches and brought into the open the different "worlds" inhabited by members of the same church. Although I moved from one of those worlds to the other when I went from being a right-wing engineer in the oil industry to a left-wing academic, my task as a comparative ethicist is to understand both worlds as fairly and accurately as possible.

2. The Role of the Canadian Churches

Complaints about the churches' role by the former director of public affairs for Arctic Gas provide a good introduction to the churches' involvement in the debate. In his book, *Super Pipe: The Arctic Pipeline, World's Greatest Fiasco?*, Earle Gray claimed that:

> It was the churches who most actively worked with and helped finance the radical leadership of the Indian Brotherhood of the Northwest Territories. In public statements, in meetings with the Prime Minister and federal cabinet, in scores of presentations before the Berger Inquiry, in appearances before the National Energy Board, the churches stated their cause in rhetoric that was too often uncompromising, strident and filled with invective. They disputed the need for northern energy supplies; they raised the spectre of ecological disaster and devastation; they displayed an emotional

xenophobia with strong inferences of domination by malignant American interests; and they accused both corporations and governments of deception and greedy motivations leading to purposeful exploitation and oppression.[16]

After grudgingly acknowledging the churches' influence, while heaping scorn on their style, Gray identified the key issue: "But most of all, in the name of a just settlement of native land claims, they demanded a moratorium on all northern development and construction of northern pipelines, a moratorium of at least ten years or however long it might take to implement a settlement."[17]

Whereas Gray emphasized the role public interest groups played in undermining the taken-for-granted assumption that a northern pipeline was both necessary and inevitable, another author, writing with financial support from the other pipeline applicant, focused attention on changes within the oil and gas industry. In his study, carried out with financial support from Foothills Pipelines Limited, Donald Peacock suggested that the serious reservations which gradually emerged regarding a northern pipeline provided further evidence that a "new capitalist development ethic" was already "unfolding in the planning and building of northern pipelines." He pointed out that for many people within the industry, as well as for native rights activists and environmentalists, "The primary issue was whether, despite the certainty of the economic benefits, the pipeline should be built at all. This was partly because of modern doubt about the value of economic progress for its own sake, and partly a fear about environmental and sociological consequences."[18]

Church members who believed that a new capitalist development ethic was emerging, and that decisions about northern development were being made responsibly by industry and government personnel, felt that the churches' call for a moratorium on pipeline construction until native claims were settled was unnecessarily one-sided and divisive. From their point of view, the church should be more pastoral in relation to government and industry personnel and less judgmental about their activities and motives. Defenders of the churches' decision to stand openly, officially and clearly on the side of the native peoples, on the other hand, were alarmed by what was going on in the North. The times called for an impassioned, prophetic denunciation of colonial patterns of development and a vision of a new sustainable way of life for southern Canadians.

As an initial simplification I am associating the pro- and anti-pipeline positions within the churches with the tension between prophetic and pastoral orientations. I do not wish to imply, of course, that prophets are not concerned about the personal faith and well-being of individuals, or that pastors are not committed to social change. The underlying questions are how prophetic and pastoral emphases were combined by different groups, what kind of prophetic witness was appropriate in particular circumstances and whose well-being evoked one's pastoral concern.[19] I will return to those questions in the conclusion. What needs to be understood for the purposes of this study is that the churches took an official stand against the pipeline and in favour of a moratorium on major resource development schemes until native claims had been satisfactorily settled. It is thus accurate to speak of the churches as allies of the natives who wanted to block the pipeline. This does not necessarily mean, however, that this "prophetic" role in relation to the dominant groups in society, which viewed the pipeline as the inevitable next step in the development of frontier resources, was the only intelligible position for Christians to support. What is interesting about the countervailing position within the churches, which was not necessarily pro-development but which was critical of the one-sidedness of the official position, is that it provided an articulation of the moral and religious justifications available to the pragmatic politicians, civil servants and business people who just wanted to get on with the job.

   Developments leading up to the churches' official pro-moratorium stance included thorough-going reassessments of relations with native peoples, the emergence of inter-church social action coalitions designed to increase the effectiveness of the churches' social justice work, and the churches' direct involvement as critics of other northern development schemes. Support for the pipeline, and in particular for the individuals responsible for providing jobs for northerners and energy supplies for southern Canadians, was also related to new developments within the churches regarding their role in the North, their ministry with native peoples, and the role of lay people in the decision-making structures of the churches. I will return to a further consideration of these developments in the following chapter. My final task in this chapter is to identify the key elements of the method being introduced for the clarification of ethical issues or for the comparative study of moralities as cultural systems.

3. Comparative Ethics and Disciplined Inquiry

The impression is sometimes given that training in ethics gives the ethicist a mandate to bring discussions to a close with authoritative pronouncements about right and wrong actions and about what ought to be done. This, in my view, is an unfortunate misunderstanding of the discipline of ethics, and of the authority legitimately claimed by its practitioners. Nicholas Wolterstorff's discussion of the governance of our thought processes provides a useful way to think about the kind of authority the comparative ethicist claims for her or his discipline.[20] In particular, Wolterstorff's distinction between "direction governance" and "acceptance governance" helps both to limit the scope of, while at the same time establishing the need for, the authority required for disciplined discourse.

Wolterstorff points out that *what we accept* as being true or right about a particular issue is always related to a range of factors, including prior conditioning, our location in the social order, the kinds of experiences we have had, what we already believe about the situation in question, our beliefs about the nature and purpose of human life and so forth. For example, during the late 1950s and early 1960s when I was working in the Alberta oil industry I would no doubt have found the case for a Mackenzie Valley pipeline far more convincing than I did in the mid-seventies. Claims about the need for the pipeline which I now greet with scepticism would then have appeared to be self-evidently true.[21]

On the other hand, *how we direct our attention* is more directly under our control. We can agree to look at a particular aspect of an issue whether or not we think that agreement can be reached regarding what ought to be believed about it. What I am assuming in this study is that disciplined inquiry presupposes the capacity for "direction governance" but it does not require "acceptance governance." The ethicist, as ethicist, does not require a mandate to make authoritative declarations regarding which beliefs ought to be accepted. The authority required for disciplined inquiry is a mutually acceptable procedural authority which can produce agreement regarding which aspect of the issue is being debated at any particular point in time.[22]

The work of comparative ethics involves shifts in attention from action to reflection, and within the reflective mode from one level or type of discourse to another. Whether we are reconstructing a debate or leading a discussion group, it is appropriate to start with initial definitions of the problem and initial responses. This initial story-telling phase is designed to provide a preliminary look at each position as a whole as background for subjecting particular claims and arguments to closer scrutiny. In a serious debate the time comes to shift from story-telling to analysis.

When the time comes to analyse particular claims it will be noticed that different kinds of claims require different treatment. In our actual debates, and in retrospective reconstructions of earlier debates such as this study, it is necessary to deal with the relationships among personal opinions, factual claims, value judgments and basic beliefs about what is ultimately true and important. How these types of claims interact will be discussed in detail in relation to particular aspects of the debate. In this chapter, as background for understanding the shift from story-telling to analysis, or from uncritical sharing to disciplined moral discourse, I will briefly introduce the fact-value problem and the way in which moral judgments can be clarified in relation to traditional ethical theories.[23]

In their highly polarized versions the pro- and anti-pipeline positions represented typical tendencies either to separate facts and values completely or to fuse them. As the outline of different stories and different definitions of the problem in Chapter 2 will illustrate, at the level of their surface encounters the defenders and critics of the pipeline were worlds apart. From the standpoint of the former it was a typical confrontation between "realists" and "idealists." The realists talked about hard facts and exhibited little initial interest in moral claims. They assumed that factual claims and value judgments should be sharply separated, and that the role of personal or private values should be kept to a minimum. Issues of public policy should be decided on the basis of validated empirical knowledge by the persons who had this knowledge and who were responsible for the policies in question. From their point of view, emotional appeals to ethical considerations simply undermined the possibility of rational, informed debate. Two University of Saskatchewan economists, for example, complained that Berger's report, "very effectively and emotionally, presented pipeline construction up the Mackenzie Valley (within ten years) as an absolute evil against which no protection would be sufficient and for which no adequate compensation could be made."[24] Arctic Gas President William Wilder and other defenders of the pipeline frequently insisted that the issue should be dealt with sanely and rationally by persons who were prepared to face the facts.[25] From the standpoint of the pipeline's critics this assumption that facts and values could be neatly separated simply obscured the value judgments that were actually being made.

Reactions against the pipeline did involve expressions of moral outrage and thorough-going denunciations. The pipeline proposal and the way of life and the personal motives of its promoters were denounced in ways that blurred the distinction between description and evaluation.[26] According to the authors of the book, *Moratorium: Justice, Energy, the North, and the Native People*, projects such as the Mackenzie Valley pipeline "are all designed to entrench the present repressive system, in which unholy alliances between the well-known vested interests combine to keep down the poor and powerless."[27] The following passage from *Moratorium* illustrates the fusion, not only of description and evaluation, but of factual claims, moral choices and religious foundations:

The situation is clear. Canada has sufficient nonfrontier gas for 60 years domestic use. Native land rights are unsettled. Environmental damage is highly probable and potentially disastrous. Surely the only responsible, the only sane, course of action, is careful, responsible decision making or, in other words, a moratorium on the southward transportation of northern fossil fuels. Instead, the federal government is in a frenzy to meet American imposed deadlines, to follow its pro-pipeline commitment to what can only be a disastrous conclusion.

This foolhardy course is more, we suggest, than a combination of errors in judgment on the part of Ottawa mandarins and petroleum industry executives. It is the inevitable result of our government sacrificing the human wellbeing of all its citizens to the idol of economic expansion, personified in this case by multinational energy corporations and the government of the United States. Most immediately that oppressive pattern of decision making threatens the Native people of the North. But it threatens the freedom of every Canadian struggling to live in a caring and sharing relationship with God's good creation and their fellow human beings.[28]

Both the separation and the fusion of facts and values undermine disciplined inquiry into the nature of our disagreements. For one group moral claims are irrelevant, while for the other side conclusions based upon moral absolutes are presented with such certainty that further debate appears to be unnecessary, if not impossible. In the course of the debate, however, the encounters between the critics and defenders of the pipeline went beyond this surface-level polarization. Although each position was centred around a particular way of defending its moral choices, beneath the surface of the highly polarized stances each side actually backed up its claims with a similar range of ethical arguments. I am not suggesting that behind all of the shouting and arguing there was a bedrock of substantive agreement or a harmonious order which everyone would finally see. On the contrary, I am assuming that substantive disagreements were real and deep-seated. What the different sides could have seen more clearly that they had in common was the framework within which different kinds of claims could be dealt with in appropriate ways.[29]

Just as there is a time to tell our stories and to speak passionately about our moral and religious convictions, there is a time to focus attention on claims about the facts. The second step of the method is called "factual clarification," in the full realization that facts are always selected and interpreted in relation to someone's perspective and interests. For purposes of analysis and debate, however, it is possible and necessary to distinguish among description, interpretation and evaluation. An important function of the various inquiries into proposals to build a pipeline was the need to test the accuracy of conflicting claims about the need for a northern pipeline (Chapter 3) and the impact of a pipeline on northern communities (Chapter 4).

The analysis of a debate involves more than clarifying and resolving conflicting claims about the facts. Ways of interpreting agreed-upon factual claims and differing evaluations of proposed actions and policies must also be included in the discussion. Although, as the analysis of the debate will show, a line can not be neatly drawn between factual and ethical clarification, it is important to be explicit about a shift in attention to the ethical dimension of a debate. The third step in the method I am using is called "ethical clarification" to indicate this shift in attention.

Different understandings of morality and different kinds of ethical arguments can be clarified in relation to traditional ethical theories. The conviction that facts and values can be clearly separated from one another, and that factual claims are objective and public while value judgments are subjective and private, has affinities with subjectivist theories of moral language. According to these theories, as A.R.C. Duncan points out, "moral judgments are not judgments at all, but either expressions of feeling or attempts to influence the feelings and conduct of other persons."[30] The persons discussed in Chapter 3 who stressed the important of "hard facts" and who insisted that conclusions about the pipeline flowed directly from such "facts" could have been presupposing either an emotivist understanding of ethics which reduces value judgments to subjective sentiments or, as we will see below, a utilitarian emphasis on consequences.

The dominant framework within which the debate proceeded, particularly before the Berger Inquiry, reflected a traditional utilitarian emphasis on consequences. The distinguishing feature of a utilitarian theory of ethical justification is "the belief that the rightness or wrongness of human actions is to be explained by reference to their results or consequences, which are judged as good or bad."[31]

The churches and the native peoples extended the dominant utilitarian framework in two directions (Chapter 5). First, their non-negotiable demand that no pipeline be built before native land claims were settled reflected a deontological commitment to the native peoples' right to self-determination. Second, conflicting claims about whether or not the pipeline proposal represented a perpetuation of a colonial pattern of development can be explored in relation to *idealist* theories. As Duncan points out, idealist theories "seek for the grounds of both the rightness of actions and the goodness of ends in their joint relation to whole patterns or ways of life."[32] Rather than using the term idealist, however, I will refer to concerns about colonial patterns of development and consumer versus conserver ways of life as the ideological dimension of the debate.

The interaction among personal opinions, factual claims, value judgments, ethical arguments and basic convictions will be a recurrent theme in each chapter. However, as I have already suggested, the different levels of clarification characterized by story-telling; factual clarification; ethical clarification; and post-ethical reflections about basic convictions, world views, styles of operation and so forth will provide a rough framework for the chapters. In Chapter 2 I will introduce the different stories and different definitions of the problem which characterized the opposing positions. In Chapter 3 the debate before the National Energy Board (NEB) over whether or not the pipeline was needed will be used to illustrate both the difficulty of getting moral issues accepted as a legitimate aspect of the work of a public inquiry, and the extent to which, in spite of its emphasis on expertise and "hard facts," moral and ideological factors were embedded in the proceedings and findings of the NEB.

Chapters 4 and 5 will deal more explicitly with value judgments and ethical arguments. The debate over the predicted impact of the pipeline on native communities will be used in Chapter 4 to show how public inquiries tend to presuppose a framework within which ethical judgments are based upon calculating consequences and balancing costs and benefits. In Chapter 5 I will show how, with Berger's support, the debate was pressed beyond the narrow limits of a consequentialist determination of costs and benefits. My focus will be on the role of the churches in raising questions about the rights of native peoples and the adequacy of a way of life based upon consumer rather than conserver values.

In Chapter 6 I will move sideways from the rigorous arguments about factual claims, moral judgments and ethical justification to what H. David Aitken has referred to as a post-ethical level of clarification.[33] This shift in attention can be thought of in different ways. In one sense it involves a return to the story-telling mode of the first level. Deeper aspects of our identities are tapped through overall assessments of what is going on, who we are, who we want to become and so forth. This level of clarification also resembles what other scholars refer to as meta-ethics or the discussion of background theories. In the context of this study it will provide the occasion to reflect explicitly on the role of religious convictions in the debate.

In the conclusion I will return to the tension between prophetic and pastoral orientations alluded to in the title. I will remind readers that analyses such as this of earlier debates should not be expected to produce easy solutions for future conflicts between prophets and pastors. There will continue to be tensions between those who stress the rights of oppressed groups and the need for radical change and those who either identify with the decision-makers in the dominant institutions of society or who are convinced that concrete efforts to reform existing institutions will both help the oppressed and disclose for public debate the way decisions are actually made. I will suggest that attempts to clarify debates can improve communication and help participants in debates to achieve more satisfying and effective levels of co-operation. Both sides could have a clearer understanding of when it is time to insist upon paying attention to the hard facts used to determine consequences, and when it is time to shift attention to the judgments that are in fact being made about conflicting rights, different ways of life, and competing visions of the future. For a summary of the relationships between different chapters and different levels of clarification, see Figure 4, below.

Chapters	Intro	Ch.1	Ch.2	Ch.3	Ch.4	Ch.5	Ch.6	Ch.7
Background	X	X						
1. Story-Telling			X					
2. Factual Clarification				X	X			
3. Ethical Clarification					X	X		
4. Post-Ethical Clarification							X	
Conclusion								X

Figure 4: Levels of Clarification within Chapters

Notes

1.   Thomas Berger, *Northern Frontier, Northern Homeland: The Report of the MacKenzie Valley Pipeline Inquiry*, vol. 1 (Ottawa: Ministry of Supply and Services Canada, 1977), p. vii. Hereafter Berger Report.

2.   William Kilbourn, *Pipeline: TransCanada and the Great Debate, A History of Business and Politics* (Toronto, Vancouver: Clarke, Irwin , 1970), pp. vii-viii.

3.   Ibid., p. 186.

4.   Ibid., p. 178.

5.   Donald Peacock, *People, Peregrines and Arctic Pipelines: The Critical Battle to Build Canada's Northern Pipelines* (Vancouver: J.J. Douglas, 1977), p. 205.

6.   François Bregha, *Bob Blair's Pipeline: The Business and Politics of Northern Energy Development Projects* (Toronto: James Lorimer, 1979), p. 9.

7.   Ibid., pp. 19-20.

8.   Ibid., p. 25.

9.   Cited in ibid., p. 27.

10. Ibid., p. 31.

11. Ibid., p. 31.

12. Berger Report, p. 207.

13. Jim Lotz, "Northern Pipelines and Southern Assumptions," *Arctic*, 30, 4 (December 1977): 204.

14. Frederick Bird, "Paradigms and Parameters for the Comparative Study of Religious and Ideological Ethics," *Journal of Religious Ethics*, 9, 2 (Fall 1981): 159-60.

15. Jon P. Gunnemann, "Human Rights and Modernity: The Truth of the Fiction of Individual Rights," *Journal of Religious Ethics,* 16, 1 (Spring 1988): 163.

16. Earle Gray, *Super Pipe: The Arctic Pipeline, World's Greatest Fiasco?* (Toronto: Griffin House, 1979), p. 147.

17. Gray, *Super Pipe*, pp. 249-50.

18. Peacock, *People, Peregrines*, p. 205.

19. "The mandate of the Division of Mission in Canada calls for *pastoral as well as prophetic leadership*. These two kinds of leadership sometimes appear to be in conflict and often create a dilemma for members and staff of the Division" *27th General Council Record of Proceedings*, August 21st-August 30, 1977, Calgary, Alberta, p. 239.

20. Nicholas Wolterstorff, *Until Justice and Peace Embrace* (Grand Rapids, Michigan: Eerdmans, 1983).

21. To use Gunnemann's term, I took for granted the "morality-in-place" of the realm of practice associated with the development of natural resources and more generally with the operations of an industrial economy. By the time I was beginning this study as a humanities professor at the University of Toronto the transition to a different way of thinking about pipelines had accompanied my shift in social location.

22. Former industry colleagues interviewed in Calgary for this study had no trouble understanding my shift in perspective or relating to the critical questions I asked them about the pipeline proposal. They would have found me unbearably ideological, however, if I had failed to exhibit any awareness of the relationship between changing careers and changing perspectives. For neither of us did this recognition simply relativize our positions and leave us with nothing further to

talk about. Rather, it served as a precondition for a serious exploration of conflicting claims.

23. For earlier attempts to describe the method I am using in this study see "Towards 'A Pedagogy for Allies of the Oppressed,' " *Studies in Religion/Sciences Religieuses*, 13, 2 (Spring 1984): 145-50; "Comparative Ethics and the MacKenzie Valley Pipeline Debate," *The Toronto Journal of Theology*, 1, 2 (Spring 1985): 242-60; and the final chapter of *Christian Faith and Economic Justice: Towards a Canadian Perspective*, ed. Cranford Pratt and Roger Hutchinson (Burlington, Ontario: Trinity Press, 1989).

24. J.C. Stabler and M.R. Olfert, "Gaslight Follies: The Political Economy of the Western Arctic," *Canadian Public Policy*, 6 (1980): 384.

25. "Comment: Arctic Gas Study's Chairman, Setting the Record Straight," *Executive*, May 1973, pp. 29-32.

26. Ironically, neither side drew attention to the "morality-in-place" of the pipeline promoters as a morality. For one side moral concerns were irrelevant, for the other side morality was missing.

27. Hugh and Karmel McCullum and John Olthius, *Moratorium: Justice, Energy, the North, and the Native People* (Toronto: Anglican Book Centre, 1977), p. 6.

28. Ibid., p. 85.

29. See Gunnemann, "Human Rights and Modernity," p. 174: "It follows from this that the moral language of any modern society must be a differentiated moral language in which the language of morality-in-place (of *telos* and virtue) exists side by side with the language of rights and of utility. A differentiated moral language is internally inconsistent—such as the conflict between rights and utility which McIntyre correctly underscores—only in an undifferentiated moral community, that is, where boundaries between differing spheres of human activity and association are not clear, and therefore where the contexts for different modes of moral language are not clear. One of the central tasks of a differentiated moral society or community would be the articulation of the differing spheres or contexts in which each language is appropriate."

30. A.R.C. Duncan, *Moral Philosophy* (Toronto: Canadian Broadcasting Corporation, 1965), p. 37.

31. Ibid., p. 11.

32. Ibid., p. 11.

33. Cited by James Gustafson in "Context vs Principles: A Misplaced Debate," *New Theology*, no. 3, ed. Martin Marty and Dean Peerman (New York: Macmillan, 1965), pp. 71-72.

Chapter 2

Different Stories,
Different Definitions of the Problem

Mr. Blair, there is a life and death struggle going on between us, between you and me. Somehow in your carpeted boardrooms, you are plotting to take away the very centre of my existence. You are stealing my soul, my spirit. . . . If you ever dig a trench through my land, you are cutting through me. . . . Don't tell me you are not responsible. You are the twentieth century General Custer. You have come to destroy the Dene nation. You are coming with your troops to slaughter us and to steal land that is rightfully ours.[1]

Mr. Commissioner, the hard fact is that without some sort of economic development, this land—this northern land, enormous, beautiful and awe-inspiring as it is—[will not support] the population of the Northwest Territories. The hard fact is that many northerners whose forebearers [sic] lived off the land do not want to go back to the traditional means of making a livelihood. The hard fact is that at present there is insufficient economic activity in the North to give the opportunity for all those who seek wage employment to fulfill themselves in these territories.[2]

A cry for justice rings out today from Native Peoples who inhabit the Canadian North. Dramatically, on a massive scale the Native Peoples of the North find themselves and their way of life being threatened by the headlong search for new energy sources on this continent.[3]

The principle of a "just settlement" for the claims of the native people has the full support of the Presbyterian Church, as of most Canadians, but not the unfortunate proposal to "stop the clock" for ten years, with all its mischievous implications.[4]

In our everyday activities it is a common experience to realize that before we react to someone's views we should find out where she or he is coming from. Sometimes, after we have carried on a fruitless argument, and have then had a chance to hear the other person's story, we have a new appreciation for what was being said. We also have a better understanding of how the other person's arguments were being defended, even if we still disagree. Part of the discipline expected of persons engaging in ethical reflection involves attempting to view each position as a whole before it is taken apart and examined piece by piece or claim by claim. The above quotations illustrate the extent to which different reactions to the pipeline proposal reflected different stories, different definitions of the problem, and different ways of speaking about what was going on. The purpose of this chapter is to begin the task of reconstructing those stories and preparing the ground for a shift in focus from story-telling to the analysis of conflicting claims.

A story-telling moment is the first step in the reflective process which begins when attention is shifted from action to reflection. In the following chapters there will be further shifts in focus as different types of moral discourse and different levels of clarification are explored. First, however, it is important to try to glimpse the different positions as wholes, that is, as living moralities characterized by complex webs of beliefs, values, assumptions, basic convictions and personal experiences. I will begin with an initial description of an exchange between a church leader and a businessman; then outline the main elements of the conflicting perspectives of Arctic Gas and Project North; and finally draw attention to significant differences in orientation and experience on the part of church leaders who defended or opposed the pipeline.

1. Church Speaks, Business Replies

A "Church Speaks—Business Replies" exchange published in the August 1978 issue of the *United Church Observer* provides a good introduction to the pro- and anti-pipeline positions. It also illustrates the difficulty of communication between persons who belong to the same church but whose basic orientations towards an issue are so different. Following a lively discussion at a meeting between church leaders and business people, the comments of one of the church leaders was published with a reply by a businessman. The articles were called, "Firmly on the side of the poor," and "Using the church to promote a one-sided economic view."[5]

The church leader claimed that the church must be faithful to the example of the Hebrew Prophets and of Jesus. They stood firmly on the side of the poor and oppressed. "The Church that does not stand within the prophetic tradition as part of its spiritual and faith commitment is not being true to its biblical roots." Therefore:

Since anything which dehumanizes another human being is always morally wrong, the Church must stand against those things, whatever the cost. Whether those being dehumanized are Canada's native people, the oppressed blacks in South Africa, people in jails and asylums in Czechoslovakia, or Moscow, or those who suffer in jails in South America, the Church has no alternative but to speak out on behalf of those who have lost, or never possessed, any levers to control the forces that are determining their destiny.[6]

The church leader insisted that he was not simply reflecting an anti-business bias. He accepted as a presupposition that "business always has been, and always will be, a part of our human scene. Wherever there is an exchange of something valued by one person for something valued by another, we have a business transaction." He believed, however, that "the Church's responsibility to exert moral influence" in relation to economic issues "does not rest solely with the men and women within the business community." Moral issues such as euthanasia and abortion are not left strictly to the medical profession. Similarly:

Economics, investments, profits, are all issues with moral implications. These cannot be left entirely to economists, brokers and bankers. While the closing down of part of the operation of Inco is largely a matter of profits, international markets, the world monetary situation and balance of payments, etc., the whole community, its education, its health, its recreation, its religion, its senior citizens and its youth are affected by what is taking place. So it cannot be a matter solely for the officials of Inco and the union.[7]

The church leader's aim was to broaden the framework within which economic issues and business decisions were discussed. What business leaders initially heard, however, was a left-wing attack on the business system itself. According to the author of "Business Replies," "There are some business people who wonder, quite sincerely, if this antagonism towards their institution is not politically motivated." They wonder if it is "part of some design of a few church leaders who have an ideology that is hostile to our economic system." He quoted with approval an article in *The Toronto Star* called "The Church seeks a heaven on earth—with a leftist tilt." In that article, Robert Nielsen suggested that:

The church has been invaded by the young graduates of the 1960's radicalism who have succeeded in influencing the leadership. They are not usually much attracted to pastoral work—offering spiritual counsel to the troubled, comforting the sick, and consoling the bereaved. They think politically, they think big and they think of collectivist corrections for man's fallen state.[8]

In a parenthetical comment, the businessman pointed out that, "In a democratic society anyone is completely free to hold such economic views and to live by them." But, he said, "it is not fair to use a nationally funded church department to propagate them." Fairness and balance were not, however, his only concerns. He also believed that his church was supporting the wrong policies. He granted the churches' right to speak out on economic issues, but he disagreed both with what was being said in his church's name and with how it was being said. He lamented the strident tone of recent criticisms of business, and worried about the consequences of the policies promoted by the churches. "The United Church, through its support of Project North, has contributed to strife in many northern villages, division among many northern people, and unemployment for large numbers of them." He agreed with the Presbyterian Superintendent of Missions that: "Instead of helping [native people] to earn their livelihood in a twentieth century wage economy, we've forced them into unemployment and bankruptcies." The problem, he insisted, is not that the church speaks out on economic issues, but that it has been promoting the wrong policies and attacking the wrong institutions. Church members "who believe in the role of large corporations . . . feel it unfair of our church to use some of our contributions to fund outright attacks on the economic philosophy that we sincerely believe to be in the best interest of Canada."[9]

The author of "Business Replies" was also distressed by the way the church leader appealed to the scriptures to support his position. His concern was that quotations from the Old and New Testaments were used "not only in an attempt to justify the right of the Church to take political action, but also to imply the correctness of that action." Quotations from the prophets calling for solidarity with the poor were used to support criticisms of northern development projects. However, could such verses not "be used quite honestly to support a variety of economic views?" In his view, the policies advocated by church leaders had contributed to "unemployment and poverty, which are grinding indeed to the poor." The business development which offered immediate hope for jobs and dignity for northern natives was being opposed by the very church leaders who claimed to be so concerned about the poor. "Is it not a bit embarrassing for the author of the foregoing article, who is one of the chief opponents of industry's role in the north, to quote Scripture telling business people that causing poverty is wrong?" The businessman's main concern, however, was that appeals to scripture could be used "to foreclose a debate before it is really underway."[10]

I will return to this exchange in Chapter 6. My limited aim in this chapter has been to show how different judgments about the pipeline were associated with different assumptions about what the native peoples wanted and needed, different evaluations of the existing economic system, different understandings of the relationship between biblical teachings and judgments about current policies, and so forth. I will continue this introductory exploration of the different stories and different definitions of the problem which characterized the debate over the pipeline proposal by looking more closely at the cases for and against the pipeline.

2. Arctic Gas vs. Project North

The major proponents of a Mackenzie Valley natural gas pipeline were the sponsoring companies and officials of Arctic Gas. With ample encouragement from the Government of Canada they took it for granted that such a project would be in the national interest. There was a widely held conviction in the early 1970s that northern gas would soon be needed by southern consumers. Since Canadian supplies and the Canadian market were too small to justify an all-Canadian line, it would be necessary to take advantage of "economies of scale." Therefore, Arctic Gas was proposing to build a 48-inch pipeline to carry 4 billion cubic feet per day of natural gas from Alaska and the Canadian far North to markets in southern Canada and the lower 48 states. The estimated cost in 1973 was $5 billion. By the time the Arctic Gas proposal was abandoned in 1977, estimates had risen to $11-$15 billion.

The Arctic Gas position was that, even though the main justification for the pipeline was southern Canada's need for Mackenzie Delta gas, in order to finance the pipeline it would be necessary to export some of the Canadian gas to the US. In a 1973 article outlining the case for the pipeline, Arctic Gas Chairman, William Wilder, pointed out that:

> In return for a commitment of some Canadian gas
> reserves that are in excess of our own needs, this country
> will obtain substantial revenues and other economic

benefits. More important, however, is the fact that Canadians will have the means of tapping the North's potential. Without a pipeline based initially on the U.S. market, Canadians will forever have to sit on their northern resources. They will remain vast but valueless without a means of transporting them, and therefore of no benefit to Canadians.[11]

Once the need for a pipeline was established, Arctic Gas turned to the question of the costs and benefits to the Canadian economy and financial markets. According to Wilder, Arctic Gas was confident that its sophisticated econometric models would:

> produce a range of economic impacts that will show academic, government and corporate economists that the project has a substantial positive impact on the economy. Impacts of particular importance to our study program include employment, national income, interest rates, inflation, GNP, balance of payments and the Canadian dollar.[12]

In addition to studies dealing with supply and demand and with the impact of a pipeline on the Canadian economy, numerous research projects were designed to answer whatever questions might be raised about "engineering, . . . ecology and the socio-economic features of the North." As far as Arctic Gas was concerned, these studies provided a solid foundation for its conviction that a pipeline could be built and operated within reasonable environmental limits with beneficial results both for the Canadian economy and for job-hungry northerners. Wilder's conclusion illustrated the confidence with which the consortium faced the coming debate:

> In summary, Canada needs a natural gas pipeline from the Arctic late in this decade. To make this possible, we will have to export a relatively small amount of our potential Mackenzie Delta reserves, provided the pipeline also transports Alaskan Gas to U.S. markets.
>
> Careful planning based on extensive research should allow us to realize this objective in such a way as to benefit all Canadians. We believe the project can be managed carefully and wisely. It is in the national interest that discussion during the coming years be based on facts rather than rumours, and that it be conducted rationally rather than emotionally.[13]

The case for building a Mackenzie Valley pipeline was based on the assumptions that it was needed; that it could be built within reasonable environmental limits; and that its benefits for all Canadians, including northern native peoples, would be greater than its costs. Critics of the pipeline proposals challenged all of these assumptions. The brief presented to the Berger Inquiry in June 1976 by Project North on behalf of its sponsoring churches provides a good illustration of the case against immediate construction of the pipeline and for a moratorium on pipeline construction until native land claims had been settled.

The Project North brief called for a moratorium on resource development projects, including the Mackenzie Valley pipeline, for two reasons. A moratorium was required to give native peoples time to achieve a satisfactory settlement of their land claims, and "to give Canadians an opportunity to work together to develop alternative lifestyles based on conserver rather than consumer attitudes."[14] The authority to speak on behalf of the churches was based on resolutions adopted by Anglican, Roman Catholic and United churches, as well as by the Canadian Council of Churches. The brief also appealed to the decision of these churches, along with the Lutherans and Presbyterians, to increase the effectiveness of their support for native peoples through their joint sponsorship of Project North. As evidence of the ecumenical consensus embodied in the brief, reference was made to the church leaders' statement, "Justice Demands Action," which had been presented to the Prime Minister and Cabinet on March 2, 1976. This statement had also called for a moratorium on major resource development projects until a number of conditions had been met, including a just settlement of native land claims.

To explain why the churches were speaking out on an issue such as the pipeline, the brief appealed to "the biblical imperatives of justice and liberation for the poor, the dispossessed and the minorities of the world (Habakkuk 2:9-10; Amos 5:7-11)." It was acknowledged that in the past the churches had become too accommodated to the established social order. They were too uncritical of:

> an order which gives more priority to economic growth
> and profit-oriented values (which are called "realities")
> and less to social justice and human dignity (which are
> called "humanitarian sentiments"). In our experience we
> are discovering that justice and human dignity are not
> the automatic by-products of such economic growth.[15]

In traditional Christian language, the brief called for repentance from sin. It insisted, however, that sin is social as well as individual:

"Most of us live in and benefit from a socio-economic situation which is *sinful*. By social sin, we mean that we create and sustain social and economic patterns of behaviour that bind and oppress, give privilege to the powerful and maintain systems of dependency, paternalism, racism and colonialism."[16]

Repentance from social sin would favour "a change of social priorities among all Canadians." This, in turn, required clarity regarding existing priorities and assumptions. A crucial assumption guiding Canadian public policy appeared to be that "our society, as it presently operates, is basically sound, and that, at most, a few adjustments are required to cope with changing conditions." Second, it appears to be assumed "that problems can be isolated and analysed and that the results can be re-integrated with other factors on the basis of rational, functional calculations."[17]

The problem with these assumptions, according to the brief, is that: "emphasis is given to continuity with present practices and rational, technical decision-making by the 'experts' [with only a] nod in the direction of citizen participation. These are assumptions that must be challenged given the existence of the serious problems of economic and cultural inequalities."[18]

In a further step towards exposing the assumptions embedded in the pipeline proposal, the brief depicted pro- and anti-pipeline forces in dramatic terms. The situation was described as a confrontation between profit-hungry corporations and an energy-hungry South, on the one hand, versus native victims of misguided notions of progress, on the other. In such a conflict, the churches were prepared to take sides in the name of justice and equality:

> For there to be equality in this struggle it is necessary
> for the churches and all other groups interested in the
> moral and ethical questions of northern development to
> stand officially, openly and clearly on the side of justice
> for and the human rights of the Native People of this
> country.[19]

The debate over the pipeline did not simply raise the question of the human and aboriginal rights of native peoples. "It is also important to consider that the Native People are on the cutting edge of turning the direction of our society's growth from materialism and consumerism to a more fundamentally human concept. In some ways the North is fighting the South's battles."[20]

The call for a moratorium was defended "not only at the moral and ethical level but at what the government and oil companies like to describe as the 'practical' or 'realistic' or 'pragmatic' level." The last part of the brief was devoted to a consideration of the objectives which should be pursued as conditions for ending the moratorium. The first objective was a just settlement of all native land claims. Settlements which extinguish native claims, like the one "negotiated" with the Indians and Inuit of Northern Quebec after construction of the James Bay hydro development project had begun, should be avoided.

> The moratorium we propose would give all groups the necessary breathing space to negotiate and realize just land claims that reflect the wishes and the aspirations of the Dene and the Inuit. Unrealistic deadlines could be avoided and discussions could take place in an open and suitable manner in the North, rather than being rushed through a purely white man's process in Ottawa or Yellowknife.[21]

A second objective involved native peoples' programs for regional political development. "The slogan of the Native People, 'Land Not Money,' reflects the desire for self-determination and control of their own destiny." This desire is both a legitimate goal in itself and a means towards survival. Economic development programs based on renewable resources and traditional activities will "have little chance of development if the Native People are attempting to adjust to, and live within, the enormous social and economic unrest of the construction period for a pipeline."[22]

Adequate safeguards "to deal with environmental problems like oil spills, blowouts, damage to the terrain and the living creatures" should be in place before major projects receive approval. "The hasty planning that has accompanied so many massive industrial and energy projects in the North exemplifies the frontier boom-or-bust mentality of colonial development." The brief argued that "a moratorium . . . should be used to change this pattern so that adequate safeguards are planned and included in proposals before the construction phase begins."[23]

Finally, the brief called for "adequate programs to regulate domestic consumption and export of energy resources." The churches were not convinced by the claims made by government and industry that frontier oil and gas were urgently needed in the South. This scepticism about the need for a pipeline, which will be explored more fully in the following chapter, was shared by other public interest groups such as Energy Probe, the Committee for an Independent Canada, the Committee for Justice and Liberty (now called Citizens for Public Justice), Oxfam, the Canadian Arctic Resources Committee and the Canadian Wildlife Federation.

The churches pointed out that the Canadian people had never received an adequate explanation of "the unbelievable discrepancy between 1971 and 1974 statements with respect to oil and gas reserves in this country." Until an independent public inquiry had produced "some straight answers on energy supply and demand so that the public can participate meaningfully in decision-making," there should be a moratorium on pipeline construction and offshore drilling. There were a number of factors which seemed to count as evidence against the claim that northern supplies were needed immediately. For example, recent studies seemed to indicate that more energy could be saved by investing in conservation measures than could be provided by spending the same amount of money on oil and gas exploration, production and transportation. If northern gas was so desperately needed in southern Canada, why was so much Alberta gas being exported to the US rather than being piped to eastern markets? "Surely the churches and Native organizations are justified in asking, 'What's the rush to build the Mackenzie Valley pipeline when there are so many unanswered questions?' "[24]

In the concluding section of the brief, the "pragmatic," "realistic" economic and environmental arguments were relocated in the context of ethical concerns and a religious vision for Canada:

> "In the final analysis," as the 1975 Roman Catholic Labour Day message reminds us, "what is required is nothing less than fundamental social change. Until we as a society begin to change our own life styles based on wealth and comfort, until we begin to change the profit-oriented priorities of our industrial system, we will continue placing exorbitant demands on the limited supplies of energy in the North and end up exploiting the people of the North in order to get those resources."[25]

This closing appeal to an alternative vision of the Canadian nation was designed to return the Commissioner's attention to the brief's earlier call for conversion. The churches' willingness to encourage an escalation of the debate into a full-blown confrontation between good and evil had been reflected in the churches' ringing declaration that:

> simple tinkering and patchwork will not suffice to bring justice to its fullest extent in our society.
> We are talking about more than simple reformism and calling for more than individual conversion. We are

calling for a conversion within our social and economic structures whereby policy making and decision making will begin to reflect and make practical the values of justice, dignity and fulfillment for every human being. Our corporate sins must be acknowledged and we must turn around, if we are to have a society that truly reflects the social consequences of the New Commandment. To bless the established order is to remain unconverted![26]

3. Conflicting Views of the North and of the Role of the Church

Both the call for a moratorium, and the way in which Project North presented its case, aroused controversy within the churches. Even the United Church, which had unhesitatingly joined the Anglican and Roman Catholic churches in the fall of 1975 to create Project North, had reservations about the demand to delay the pipeline for ten years. Among the church leaders who found the case for a northern pipeline compelling were two Presbyterians who attended the University of Alberta's Arctic Summer School (June 18-July 2, 1976). Lengthy reports by George A. Johnston and Alex. F. MacSween reflected the standpoint of southern Canadians who took it for granted that the North was, as Johnston suggested in the title of his report, Canada's emerging new frontier.

There is always an interesting relationship between the views one holds and the kinds of experiences one has had. It is tempting, on the one hand, to conclude that one goes looking for the experiences that will confirm the beliefs and assumptions one already has. On the other hand, we sometimes assume that the views one holds are the result of particular experiences. For the purposes of improving communication between opposing camps, it is enough to notice that our ideas and our experiences are interrelated. What we experience influences what we believe; what we believe affects the decisions we make about the kinds of situations in which we place ourselves. There was a very evident fit between the beliefs and commitments which prompted Hugh and Karmel McCullum to go to work for Project North and the experiences they had and the people they met while travelling in the North. There was a similar fit between the beliefs and commitments which prompted George Johnston and Alex MacSween to attend a course sponsored and staffed by promoters of the pipeline and the experiences they had and the people they met.

While carrying out research for their book, *This Land Is Not For Sale*, the McCullums travelled thousands of miles across the North. The more they travelled, and the more they observed the impact upon native communities of development schemes such as the Manitoba Hydro Churchill River diversion scheme, the James Bay Project in northern Quebec, logging in British Columbia and mining in Labrador, the more convinced they became that it would be wrong to build the pipeline, especially before native land claims were settled. The North they studied was the homeland of the natives, and it was the original inhabitants who must be allowed to decide what they wanted to do and to become.

As participants in the University of Alberta's Arctic Summer School, Johnston and MacSween studied the other North. Their North, and the North of Arctic Gas, had been described in the Robert Service poem MacSween used as a prologue for his report. The following lines from "The Law of the Yukon" picture a wilderness waiting to be conquered:

I am the land that listens, I am the land that broods;
Steeped in eternal beauty, crystalline waters and woods.
Long have I waited lonely, shunned as a thing accurst,
Monstrous, moody, pathetic, the last of the lands and the first.
Visioning camp-fires at twilight, sad with a longing forlorn,
Feeling my womb o'er pregnant with the seed of cities unborn.
Wild and wide are my borders, stern as death is my sway,
And I wait for the men who will win me—and I will not be
     won in a day;
And I will not be won by weaklings, subtle, suave and mild,
But by men with the hearts of vikings, and the simple faith of
     a child.
Desperate, strong and relentless, unthrottled by fear of defeat,
Them will I gild with my treasure, them will I glut with my
     meat.

In the final lines of his poem, Service has the North dreaming:

Of cities leaping to stature, of fame like a flag unfurled,
As I pour out my tide of riches in the eager lap of the world.[27]

This view of the North as "the last frontier" both shaped and was shaped by a positive attitude towards the pipeline, a negative attitude towards the call for a moratorium on pipeline construction until native claims had been settled, and a particular set of assumptions about the role of the churches in the North. The overwhelming impression received by MacSween and Johnston during their trip to the North was that natives and whites wanted development and rejected the churches' call for a moratorium. The persons with whom they spoke accused southern church leaders of adopting a moratorium policy without consultation with northerners. Members of the churches sponsoring Project North were particularly annoyed because they had never been given a chance to make their views known. Leaders and supporters of Project North, on the other hand, defended their decision to be in solidarity with the native leaders who were demanding a moratorium. They were convinced of the rightness of this stance, and they could point to resolutions adopted by the sponsoring denominations supporting the call for a moratorium.

In its statements and actions Project North stressed the prophetic mandate of the churches to seek justice and to take the side of powerless groups in their struggles with established power. MacSween and Johnston did not reject this view of the church, but they did not believe that such a mandate made it necessary to be totally alienated from existing mainstream institutions of society or from the routine pastoral responsibilities of the churches. When they thought about the role of their church in the North, the first thing that came to mind was the realization that the Anglican, Roman Catholic and United churches "should not be expected any longer to carry the whole burden of Christian witness in the far north."[28] In keeping with the ecumenical spirit, which was also reflected in the inter-church social action coalitions such as Project North, they wondered what special task there might be for Presbyterians in the North. On the one hand, the number of Presbyterians they met, including natives raised Presbyterian in Alaska, suggested that it might be time to establish Presbyterian congregations in the larger communities. On the other hand, there seemed to be a need for and an interest in ministers to serve in "the drilling camps, base camps and other population centres in the Delta area."[29]

There were counselling and educational needs which could be met by the right kind of person. As MacSween said:

> The missionary would need to be a man able to maintain a balanced perspective, and if he is to be of any real help will need to be interested in "people" rather than in issues. The said minister might well operate on the same schedule as most of the men, spending two or three weeks in the north, then a week or so "outside" at his home, presumably in Edmonton. It was suggested to us that the Companies concerned could readily provide transportation to and from Edmonton via their own regularly scheduled passenger aircraft, as well as suitable accommodation and hospitality while in the Camps. If and when construction

on a pipeline commences, and work in other potential industries, there will be additional camps where such a ministry would be welcomed, provided of course, in all cases, the missionary was the right type of person. No one else should be considered.[30]

Johnston also stressed the importance of co-ordinating Presbyterian activities with other mission work in the North. He pointed out that there seemed to be ample opportunities to worship and to participate in religious activities in population centres such as Aklavik, but he agreed with MacSween that there were unfulfilled needs in the work camps. He reported that:

When approached about the possibilities of an itinerant mission to the men, the Director of Corporate Affairs . . . of one of the large oil firms remarked, "You know, we figured we had thought of everything for our men, but we didn't think of that. I'm intrigued with the idea." He went on to explain how he had appreciated the padre's hour in the armed services. A promise was made to discuss the matter with officials higher up in the organization. Hopefully, it will not end there, but may lead eventually to the opening of a beneficial ministry.[31]

Most social activists would recoil from the image of industry-sponsored ministers playing the same role in work camps that chaplains play at military bases or in correctional institutions. It was, and is, very difficult for persons who inhabit these different worlds to have fruitful debates about the nature of the North, the meaning of the pipeline proposal and the role of the churches in the North. The task of the comparative ethicist is not primarily to reconcile such differences. The differences might very well be irreconcilable as far as church policy is concerned. In the past, schisms have resulted from disagreements about the nature and purpose of a particular church's mission and identity which were no more basic than the differences dividing defenders and opponents of the pipeline proposal. The aim is to clarify issues and to improve the quality of debate. An important side-effect could be a renewed willingness to work together in spite of deeply held differences and to see that the whole mission of the churches involves both prophetic and pastoral emphases.

Whether or not the desire to provide counselling and educational services and opportunities to worship for the camp personnel is in itself inconsistent with a prophetic, social justice understanding of the Christian faith is an interesting question. I will return in the conclusion to the tension between prophetic and pastoral orientations, and to the importance of being concrete and contextual in our judgments about one another's policies and activities. My next task is to move from story-telling to analysis by looking more closely at the factual claims, moral judgments and ethical arguments used by each side to support its conclusion that the pipeline should or should not be built.

Notes

1. "Statement to the MacKenzie Valley Pipeline Inquiry: Frank T'Seleie, Fort Good Hope, 5 August 1975," in *Dene Nation—The Colony Within*, ed. Mel Watkins (Toronto and Buffalo: University of Toronto Press, 1977): 16.

2. Pierre Genest, Arctic Gas lawyer to the MacKenzie Valley Pipeline Inquiry, cited in Martin O'Malley, *The Past and Future Land: An Account of the Berger Inquiry into the MacKenzie Valley Pipeline* (Toronto: Peter Martin Associates, 1976): 1-2.

3. Canadian Conference of Catholic Bishops, *Northern Development: At What Cost?* (Ottawa: Canadian Conference of Catholic Bishops, 1975 Labour Day Statement).

4. Rev. Alex. F. MacSween, "A Journey to Northern Canada: Midsummer, 1976," unpublished Report to the Board of World Mission, The Presbyterian Church in Canada, October 1976, p. 68.

5. W. Clarke MacDonald, "Church Speaks: 'Firmly on the Side of the Poor,'" and Ronald G. Willoughby, "Business Replies: 'Using the Church to Promote a One-sided Economic View,'" *United Church Observer*, August 1978, pp. 16-18 and 19-21.

6. Ibid., pp. 17-18.

7. Ibid., p. 16.

8. Cited in "Business Replies," p. 21.

9. Ibid., p. 20.

10. Ibid., p. 21.

11. William Wilder, "Canada Needs the Arctic Pipeline," *The Financial Post*, 27 October 1973, p. C-2.

12. Ibid., p. C-2.

13. Ibid., p. C-2.

14. Project North, "A Call for a Moratorium: Some Moral and Ethical Considerations Relating to the MacKenzie Valley Pipeline," reprinted in *Canadian Churches and Social Justice*, ed. John R. Williams (Toronto: Anglican Book Centre and James Lorimer, 1984), p. 156.

15. Ibid., p. 157.

16. Ibid., p. 157.

17. Ibid., pp. 157-58.

18. Ibid., p. 158.

19. Ibid., p. 161.

20. Ibid., p. 161.

21. Ibid., p. 162.

22. Ibid., pp. 162-63.

23. Ibid., p. 163.

24. Ibid., p. 165.

25. Ibid., p. 167.

26. Ibid., p. 158.
27. MacSween, "Journey to Northern Canada," p. b.
28. Ibid., p. 71.
29. Ibid., p. 71.
30. Ibid., p. 71.
31. George A. Johnston, "A Look at Canada's Emerging Frontier," A Report to the Board of World Mission, the Presbyterian Church in Canada on the Arctic Summer School, University of Alberta, June 18-July 2, 1976, and the Canadian Northwest, Edmonton 1976, p. 9.

Chapter 3

"Hard Facts"
and the Need for a Northern Pipeline

In response to Project North's June 1976 brief to the Berger Inquiry, the President of Arctic Gas complained that "few people like to face the facts, particularly about the pipeline."[1] He was convinced that Canada's national well-being required immediate access to Mackenzie Delta gas, and that opposition was based on ignorance. A letter in the Anglican national paper expressed a similar view: "It is bad enough that these churchmen should be helping to split Canada into opposing factions, but to 'bomb out' with inaccurate information and childish advice will not help the Anglican image."[2] During the height of the debate an Edmonton journalist reported that, "anti-pipeline church action groups—such as the inter-church organization Project North—are coming under fire from those who say that pulpit preaching and pipeline planning make an ill-fated communion of interests."[3]

A common criticism of the church leaders' involvement in the pipeline debate was that they were well-intentioned but ill-informed. In their legitimate desire to support native peoples in their struggle for a just settlement of their land claims they were, according to their critics, more influenced by their prejudgments and anti-business bias than by "hard facts." From Project North's point of view, it was the pipeline's defenders who were unwilling to look at the hard facts about whether or not the pipeline was needed and what impact it would have on native communities and the Canadian economy. They were afraid that government and industry representatives would remain captivated by the taken-for-granted assumption that a Mackenzie Valley pipeline would be the next inevitable step in the development of frontier resources. Was it not possible that a pro-development bias would prompt pro-pipeline forces to ignore such "hard facts" as that the pipeline was not needed and that its costs would far outweigh its benefits?

In this chapter the question of whether or not the pipeline was needed will be examined with two concerns in mind. First, how did the churches and other public interest groups back up their argument that the pipeline was not needed? Did they base this conclusion on answers to technical questions such as the amount of gas available from western Canada, the amount of gas discovered in the North, and the rate at which these reserves could be delivered to market? Or, did they primarily argue that the pipeline ought not to be built even if there appeared to be a need in southern Canada for northern gas?

Since the churches did, in fact, argue on highly technical grounds that the pipeline would not be needed for a number of years, the initial task at this level of clarification involves examining the claims and counter-claims of the opposing sides. What claims about reserves, deliverability rates, energy needs, and so forth did the pipeline's proponents make that the critics challenged, and vice versa? A second step involves making the transition from factual to ethical clarification, or from describing to interpreting and evaluating. Although the National Energy Board focused attention on technical questions such as the supply and demand of natural gas, its conclusions embodied assumptions about whose way of life should be protected, and how costs and benefits should be distributed. Thus, the twofold aim of this chapter is to show how the debate over whether or not the pipeline was needed involved both disagreement about the facts and different assumptions about how the facts should be interpreted and how the options should be evaluated.

1. "What Is the Rush?"

The initial concern of the churches, as outlined in the 1976 Project North brief to the Berger Inquiry, was that it was very difficult for ordinary Canadians to decide whether or not there were shortages or surpluses of oil and natural gas, whether import controls should be strengthened or relaxed, or whether a northern pipeline was needed immediately. They complained that conflicting reports about natural gas supply and demand had left Canadians in a state of confusion. The Honourable Joe Greene, Minister of Energy, Mines and Resources, had assured Canadians in 1971 that we had a 923-year supply of oil and a 392-year supply of gas. He argued that Canada "had better export these non-renewable resources before they became obsolete." By 1974, when interest had shifted from larger exports to the possibility of a northern pipeline, the National Energy Board concluded that Canada would be a net importer of oil by 1982. And, "of course, the applicants before this inquiry and the same Department of Energy, Mines and Resources insist that a natural gas shortage is just around the corner." The churches believed that:

> Nothing short of a full and independent public inquiry
> will ever serve to give the people of the country the facts
> they need to make the decisions about what is and what
> is not in their interests. And until such a public inquiry

produces some straight answers on energy supply and
demand so that the public can participate meaningfully
in decision-making, a moratorium on offshore drilling
and pipeline construction should be in force.[4]

The churches were convinced that if the federal government
would take the appropriate steps there would be sufficient supplies of
natural gas to meet Canadian needs until at least the year 2001. They
presented four arguments to back up this claim. First, as a 1975
Science Council of Canada study pointed out, the projected amount of
natural gas consumed in 1995 could be reduced by thirty per cent if a
serious program of waste reduction was begun immediately. Four years
could be added to natural gas supply projections by such cutbacks in
consumption.

A second way to postpone the date by which northern gas would
be needed would be to see that Canada's existing twelve-year supply,
which Arctic Gas agreed was available, was delivered to the consumers
who needed it. "The main problem is not availability but *deliverability*
and the main reason for this is that TransCanada Pipelines cannot
meet eastern Canadian demands because the Crown-owned
corporation is unwilling to pay the price suppliers are asking for
available Alberta natural gas."[5]

The churches' third argument was related to natural gas exports
to the United States. In 1976 Canada was exporting one trillion cubic
feet per year, or forty per cent of Canada's annual production.
Contracts had been negotiated for the delivery of an additional
fourteen trillion cubic feet between 1974 and 1995. However,
"reduction or elimination of exports is allowable under Canadian law
if supply conditions warrant."[6] Canada's natural gas supply could be
extended by seven years if ten trillion cubic feet were diverted from
exports to domestic use.

Finally, the churches pointed out that approximately three years
could be added to future supplies by accepting the offer of the Alberta
government to sell more Alberta gas to eastern consumers in return for
an equivalent amount of northern gas in the future. In total, therefore,
the twelve-year supply in existing reserves already available for
Canadian consumers, the four years added through conservation, the
seven years gained through export cutbacks, and the three years added
by promising to replace Alberta gas in the future amounted to a
twenty-six-year supply of non-northern gas. Therefore, since a northern
pipeline would not be needed before the end of the century, the
churches felt justified in asking, "What's the rush to build the
Mackenzie Valley Pipeline when there are so many unanswered
questions?"[7]

2. Public Interest Groups and the National Energy Board

The argument over whether or not the pipeline was needed must be seen as a part of the larger debate about whether or not the pipeline ought to be built. On the one hand, a convincing case that the pipeline was not needed should have had a decisive impact upon the debate about whether or not it should be built. On the other hand, even if a strong case could be made regarding the need for the pipeline, there could be other overriding grounds for deciding not to build it. The churches' main reasons for asking for a moratorium were to allow time for a satisfactory settlement of native claims and to give Canadians time to adapt to the change from consumer to conserver attitudes. During the period of the moratorium four objectives should be actively pursued: the settlement of all native land claims; the development of native peoples' programs for regional economic development; the design of adequate safeguards to deal with environmental problems like oil spills, blowouts, damage to the terrain and to the living creatures; and, the development of adequate programs to regulate domestic consumption and export of energy resources. The churches' views about supply and demand projections, and about the need for a public inquiry into Canada's energy policies, were expressed in the context of the final objective.

The churches had hoped for a more open and accessible forum than the National Energy Board so that the full range of questions regarding the production, consumption and export of oil and natural gas could be explored. However, since it was the responsibility of the National Energy Board to assess the evidence regarding whether or not a pipeline was needed, the Board hearings became the main setting for that aspect of the debate. Between April 12, 1976, and May 12, 1977, the Board held 204 days of public hearings to consider six different proposals for delivering northern gas to southern markets. Although neither Project North nor any of its sponsoring churches applied for intervener status before the Board, they had close working relations with some of the groups which did, particularly the Committee for Justice and Liberty (CJL). This group later changed its name to Citizens for Public Justice (CPJ). CJL's Research and Policy Director, John Olthuis, worked closely with Project North throughout the period of the pipeline debate. He played a crucial role at the NEB hearings, and he has served as the lawyer for a number of native bands in different parts of the country. The other groups which applied for intervener status were the Canadian Arctic Resources Committee, Canadians for Responsible Northern Development, the Canadian Wildlife Federation, the Committee for an Independent Canada, the

Consumers' Association of Canada, Energy Probe, and the York University Working Group on Canadian Energy Policy.

At the May 6, 1976, meeting of the Project North Administrative Committee, representatives from the Committee for Justice and Liberty outlined their plans for the National Energy Board hearings. The federal government was continuing to push the Arctic Gas proposal in spite of new reserves in Alberta and Saskatchewan. Even pipeline companies such as Alberta Gas Trunk, Alcan and Foothills now admitted that natural gas reserves in the western provinces gave southern Canada a thirty-four- year supply. The "public interest criteria" in relation to which CJL would seek to prove that the best interests of Canadians would not be served by a northern pipeline covered the same concerns outlined in the Project North brief to the Berger Inquiry. The two organizations agreed to continue to work closely together in relation to both the Berger and NEB hearings.

The main aim of the public interest groups which participated in the National Energy Board hearings was to challenge the basic assumption that the pipeline was needed. They were well aware that they were up against both an overwhelming amount of highly technical data in support of the different applications and a pervasive sense of the inevitability of a northern pipeline. Unless this aura of inevitability was shattered, the pipeline debate would remain at the level of a narrowly technical discussion about which proposal ought to be endorsed. In the fall of 1975 the public interest groups had challenged the taken-for-granted framework and ethos within which government officials, industry representatives and the NEB usually handled questions of Canada's energy policies. They questioned the suitability of Marshall Crowe to chair the pipeline hearings. As chairman of the Canada Development Corporation he had played an active part in gaining federal government support for the Arctic Gas proposal. Before the NEB hearings opened in October 1975, Arctic Gas had asked him to step aside so that the question of his objectivity would not arise. Crowe was offended by the suggestion, but he agreed to open the hearings with a clear statement of his position. It was a compromise that Arctic Gas would later regret.

When each intervener was asked to respond to Crowe's position, five of the eighty-nine parties recognized by the Board objected. The objectors were the public interest groups named above. The case was referred to the Federal Court, which decided that Crowe could continue to sit. That decision was appealed to the Supreme Court of Canada by the Committee for Justice and Liberty, the Canadian Arctic Resources Committee and the Consumers' Association of Canada. In March 1976 the Supreme Court concluded that:

the participation of Mr. Crowe in the discussions and
decisions leading to the application made by Canadian
Arctic Gas Pipeline Limited for a certificate of public
convenience and necessity . . . cannot but give rise to a
reasonable   apprehension,   which   reasonably   well-
informed persons could properly have, of a biased
appraisal and judgment of the issue to be determined.[8]

A new panel was appointed with Jack Stabback as chairman and
hearings started over again in April 1976. Apart from the excitement
the David and Goliath contest generated among the supporters of the
public interest groups, the main impact of the court action was on the
timing of the NEB hearings. The six-month delay put the Canadian
regulatory   process   behind   the   corresponding   Federal   Power
Commission hearings in the United States. This put the Board under
heavy pressure to reach a decision before the Americans gave up on
the idea of using a pipeline to transport Alaskan gas to the southern
states. An alternative was to liquefy the natural gas and ship it south
in tankers. Even more threatening to the Arctic Gas proposal was the
emergence of an application to ship Alaskan gas along the Alaska
Highway instead of up the Mackenzie Valley. Mackenzie Delta and
Beaufort Sea gas could be linked at a later date by building a smaller
pipeline along the Dempster Highway. The delay in the hearings gave
Foothills (Yukon) enough time to prepare what turned out to be the
successful proposal.

3. The Decision-Making Process of the NEB

Although a narrowly technical framework characterized the Board's
handling of the arguments about supply and demand, its overall
approach was very comprehensive. In addition to the chapters on
supply and demand and engineering design and technical feasibility,
the three-volume report included chapters on contractual, financial and
economic matters, regional socio-economic impact and environmental
impact. Furthermore, Board members were fully aware that issues such
as the settlement of native land claims and the US desire to have
immediate access to Alaskan gas influenced the milieu in which the
hearings were taking place. The Board took great care to outline the
process by which it normally reached its conclusions and to explain the
modifications which were required in this particular case.[9]
     Decisions about a pipeline application are usually made by
focusing on six inter-related factors. First, evidence must be presented
to establish that present and probable reserves justify the capital and

operating costs. These reserves form the basis for predicting deliverability schedules. Producer-shipper contracts based on these deliverability schedules should be presented along with the application. These contracts, in turn, provide the basis for contracts between the shippers and the pipeline companies. The transportation contracts form the basis for predicting the costs and rate of return for the pipeline company. And, finally, "producer-shipper contracts and transportation contracts form the basis of the financing of the pipeline and are usually required to be pledged as security for the debt to be issued."[10]

In the case of the proposals for a Mackenzie Valley pipeline this sequence could not be followed. Since drilling was going on in the Mackenzie Delta while the hearings were proceeding, the Board was prepared to go ahead on the assumption that sufficient gas would be found to justify Canadian participation in a pipeline designed to carry Alaskan and Canadian gas to southern markets. However, by the time the hearings ended only 5.3 trillion cubic feet had been discovered. What further perplexed the Board was that even this small amount had not been protected for Canadian customers.

> Several years ago the producers had contracted the gas they expected to find in the Delta to United States buyers in exchange for funds advanced by companies for exploration and development programs in the Delta. However, the Board's report in 1975 on the Supply and Demand Requirements for Natural Gas issued after lengthy public hearings, made it evident that there was no prospect of exports from the initial reserves discovered in the Delta. Despite the fact that over two years have passed, the disengagement from United States contracts had not been completed when the hearings ended and contracts with Canadian shippers had not come into effect and could not be examined. *The Board has difficulty understanding why the producers failed to provide the evidence on one of the most vital links in the chain for a project in which they were the sponsors* [emphasis added].[11]

The Board acknowledged the uncertainties facing the companies, but concluded that "the actions of the producers in the Delta have not been conducive to an orderly decision-making process in such a large and complex project of national and international scope."[12] By contracting more gas to US buyers than had been discovered in the Delta the companies sponsoring the Arctic Gas proposal left the Board with no choice but to conclude that their application was not in the public interest. The Board did not, however, become convinced that a northern pipeline was not needed. It added its support to the Foothills (Yukon) proposal to follow the Alaska Highway. An examination of the Board's response to the arguments presented by the public interest groups will illustrate both the debate over the facts about supply and demand, and the way in which each side made different assumptions about what can and ought to be done about the energy needs of southern Canadians.

4. The NEB and the Arguments of the Public Interest Groups

The first argument, that conservation measures could lead to energy savings which could delay the need for northern gas, had been promoted by public interest groups such as the churches, the Committee for Justice and Liberty, and Energy Probe for two reasons. Less wasteful use of non-renewable resources was the right thing to do, and it was a means to extend the life of existing supplies of oil and gas. In order to meet lower consumption targets, the public interest groups were willing to force Canadians to adapt to lower levels of natural gas consumption by allowing shortages to occur. According to the Board, conservation alone would not close the gap between supply and demand. "New supplies will be needed to replace the declining deliverability of oil and gas from the Western Provinces."[13]

The Board recognized that restricting supply does reduce demand. That fact had been dramatically illustrated in the period following the creation of the Organization of Oil Producing Countries (OPEC),which led to a sudden increase in the price of Middle East oil. To plan such reductions in supply would, according to the Board, infringe upon "the choices freely made by the public at large." As it pointed out:

> conservation is a complex issue not solely related to policies of federal and provincial governments for the encouragement of restraint and curtailment of demand, but more importantly to choices freely made by the public at large on life styles and on social goals, as well as to economic considerations. Changes normally proceed more slowly than some elements in society wish, and the Board under the National Energy Board Act clearly has no mandate to force changes in the manner sought by some interest groups. Rather, the Board has sought to perceive the rate of change which will probably occur in the complex milieu of Canadian

society and to reflect this perception in its forecast of demand.[14]

The churches, on the other hand, assumed that it was the native peoples who should be given time to adjust to the changes which would accompany pipeline construction. Questions such as whose way of life ought to be protected and who should be forced to adapt to changes were not, however, easily addressed within the National Energy Board's frame of reference.

The second argument was related to the question of the availability and deliverability of natural gas to Canadian consumers. The most ambitious attempt to counteract the supply and demand projections used by government and industry to justify immediate construction of a northern pipeline was carried out by John Helliwell, a University of British Columbia economist. As François Bregha points out, Helliwell's "extensive computer modelling of natural gas supply and demand indicated that there would be no need for frontier gas until the early 1990s." According to Bregha, although officials in the Privy Council and the Department of Energy, Mines and Resources took Helliwell's findings very seriously, "the N.E.B. did not seem prepared to accept the implications of Helliwell's conclusions." He suggests that it was "the Board's obvious prejudgment of the issue" which evoked the following comment from Helliwell:

> It was increasingly clear that the evidence from the model was not acceptable to the N.E.B., and that great efforts would be made by the N.E.B. to discredit the evidence from the model and to permit the N.E.B. to continue to conclude that gas from the frontier regions would be needed in the early 1980s.[15]

From the Board's point of view, Helliwell's model failed to take into account a number of factors which increased the uncertainty of all supply projections. For example, it was misleading "to imply that the gas industry operates as if controlled by a single decision maker."

> Such an illusion is dangerous and completely at odds with the reality of the imperfections in industry decision making, with the political reality that objectives of producing and consuming provinces do not always coincide. It ignores the fact that the hundreds of existing gas purchase contracts result in inflexibility, and that provinces have protection formulae for reserves required to meet the provinces' future needs. Models generate

> instantaneous results and decisions regardless of the
> presence or absence of all the facts, or the accuracy
> thereof. In reality, it takes time to make decisions, and
> this is aptly illustrated by the applications now before us;
> models, while valuable in providing insights into the
> future, cannot be expected to include all the
> complexities of real life situations.[16]

The Board admitted that the task of deciding if or when a
northern pipeline would be needed was "bedeviled by the inability to
accurately predict demand and supply." Furthermore, long lead times
between the inception and completion of projects, the severe cold of
Canadian winters and "the lessons from recent shortages of natural gas
suffered by our neighbour to the south" provided additional reasons
for being cautious. Such factors "make it prudent for Canada to
provide for itself a safety margin in connecting new sources of supply
earlier than uncertain forecast may indicate a need."[17] As I suggested
above, the Board's caution on behalf of southern Canadians and their
southern neighbours involved moral and political judgments regarding
whose way of life should to be allowed to evolve in accordance with
their own needs and who must be prepared to adapt to changes forced
upon them by others. This was not, however, the type of question that
could be easily debated within the framework taken for granted by the
Board.

The argument that exports should be reduced immediately in
order to reserve this gas for Canadian use was firmly rejected by the
Board. Interveners argued that the date at which frontier gas would be
required by southern Canadians could be delayed if the fourteen
trillion cubic feet of gas scheduled for export to the United States
between 1977 and 1990 were reduced or cut off altogether. A Board
study, however, comparing deliverability rates from western Canadian
reservoirs with and without exports after 1977, demonstrated to the
Board's satisfaction that in both cases Canadian demand for natural
gas would catch up to supply by 1990. Therefore, cancelling export
licences would not affect the date by which a northern pipeline would
be needed.

At first glance this surprising finding appeared to be based
primarily on expert knowledge about the actual performance of natural
gas reservoirs. The Board stated that, "The reason [northern gas will
be needed by 1990 whether or not exports are curtailed] is that
because of reservoir characteristics a unit of production foregone early
in the production history of a pool can be produced later only at
reduced rates, over a longer period of time."[18] In making this
statement, the Board was challenging both the common sense view of

non-experts who thought in terms of total amounts of available gas and the submission of one of the expert witnesses called by the Committee for Justice and Liberty. What is interesting in this context is the weight the Board attached to the expertise required to calculate deliverability rates and the way in which attention was directed away from other equally crucial factors.

The Committee for Justice and Liberty had decided to back up its claim that the pipeline would not be needed until the end of the century by calling its own expert. Dalhousie economist Michael Bradfield was asked to report on the sophisticated statistical studies he had carried out on the industry's natural gas supply data. His findings indicated that cutting off exports would postpone the date by which Canadian demand for natural gas would catch up to supply. However, underlying his supply projections was the assumption that a given amount of gas not produced early in the life of a reservoir could be delivered to market at the same rate at a later date. This was not necessarily a faulty assumption if Bradfield believed that some Alberta or Saskatchewan fields would remain completely shut in until they were needed. They would then be expected to deliver gas to market at the new reservoir rate. A more important consideration is whether deliverability rates were the most important factor in the final determination of supply and demand projections.

For the Board, deliverability rates were crucial, and faulty assumptions about them were fatal to the credibility of a witness. The Board pounced on Bradfield's admission that he had not studied the behaviour of actual gas pools. "Perhaps more importantly, Dr. Bradfield acknowledged having no expertise in the field of reservoir engineering."[19] Consequently, his projections were not simply modified, they were completely discredited.

> In the case of Dr. Bradfield, who appeared on behalf of CJL, it is apparent from the evidence adduced in cross-examination that he has given little, if any, consideration to either the technical or economic feasibility of developing deliverability in the purely numerical exercise that he undertook for presentation at the hearing. In the view of the Board, Dr. Bradfield's unfamiliarity with basic gas supply concepts and supply/demand interactions, has led to faulty assumptions and erroneous conclusions; making his assessment of the possible range of shortfall dates inaccurate.[20]

The Board was rigorous and thorough when it came to exposing Helliwell's and Bradfield's lack of expertise in reservoir engineering.

There were other factors, however, which had more bearing than deliverability projections on their conclusion that a pipeline was needed immediately. For example, the Board based its predictions about the rate at which natural gas could be delivered to market "on the likelihood that there would be a significant reduction in drilling and exploration activity in Alberta in the absence of the prospect of early cash returns and that the industry decision-making process would, in these circumstances, be slowed down."[21] The Board could have based its projections on the likelihood that the federal government would nationalize the oil and natural gas industry and thus ensure exploration and production schedules designed to meet Canadian energy needs rather than to maximize corporate profits. The National Energy Program and Petro-Canada did appear on the scene within a few years as part of the government's effort to regain a degree of Canadian control over Canadian resources. My point is not that the Board ought to have extended the discussion in such an explicitly political direction. Rather, I am drawing attention to the assumptions which were in fact being made about the relationships between market forces, the power of multinational oil companies and government willingness to intervene in the economy. The Board's preoccupation with technical aspects of the issue both obscured the existence of these assumptions and made it difficult for public interest groups to shift attention to such ethical and political dimensions of the debate.

In the final analysis, the possibility of restricting exports was simply dismissed:

> In any case, the Board regards it as quite unrealistic to think that the Canadian Government would cut off exports of natural gas in their entirety at this time, when gas to meet these requirements is available. In the face of shortages and hardships in the United States clearly in evidence last winter, and which are likely to become more acute until Prudhoe Bay gas is connected, the Board could not recommend such action.[22]

The fourth argument used by the churches and other public interest groups to support their claim that a northern pipeline was not needed immediately was that Alberta might agree to sell more of its surplus gas to other Canadians in return for guaranteed access to northern reserves in the future. The Board agreed with the public interest groups that Alberta would probably make more natural gas available for central Canadian consumers. The Board assumed that "the Alberta Government would not likely foster the earliest possible connection of Delta gas since this could cause the shut-in of some

Alberta gas." In view of that fact, and considering "the pressure of Alberta producers to remove more gas from the province in order to provide more cash for exploration it seems reasonable to anticipate some relaxation of restrictions by the Government of Alberta."[23]

However, the Board's cautious approach and the federal government's desire to have access to natural gas that did not require dealings with Alberta were also reflected in comments about increased supplies from Alberta. Interveners who argued that Delta gas need not be connected until reserves in the western provinces were exhausted were firmly refuted. "While this view might have some purely economic support, the Board considers it to be wise strategy to have the ability to draw on alternative sources of supply."[24] This caution on behalf of southern Canadians demonstrates once again the crucial role of assumptions about whose way of life should be protected against the inconvenience of energy shortages and who must be prepared to adapt to the disruptive impact of pipeline construction.

5. Need, Feasibility and Desirability

The Board also pointed out, as part of its attempt to rebut arguments that the pipeline was not needed, that a decision to build the pipeline would benefit both southerners who needed the gas and northerners who needed the jobs connected with oil and gas exploration and production. A decision to delay construction of a pipeline to carry Delta gas south would discourage oil and gas exploration activity in the Western Arctic. "This would probably destabilize employment in that area, reinstitute the 'boom and bust' cycle, and eliminate or severely reduce one of the major activities contributing to steady wage employment in the Delta and nearby areas."[25] This line of argument represented a shift in focus from whether or not the pipeline was needed, and whether or not it would be feasible to finance and build such a pipeline, to what impact it would have on the Canadian economy and on native communities. Such a shift in focus serves as a reminder that whether or not the pipeline was needed was only one of the inter-related factors that entered into the Board's complex decision-making process. The need for southern access to northern gas did not stand alone as the single decisive factor determining whether or not approval should be granted for its construction. Whether the need for the pipeline was sufficiently great to justify its negative impacts would in the final analysis depend upon other factors.

Although the NEB acknowledged the full range of factors which would enter into a final decision about the desirability of the pipeline, there was a tendency for Board members to exaggerate the relevance and the authority of the kind of technical expertise required to deal with questions about supply and demand and about construction and financial feasibility. On the one hand, insofar as the public interest groups made claims about deliverability rates, it was legitimate for the Board to challenge those claims on the basis of expert knowledge about the actual performance of natural gas reserves. On the other hand, there was a striking discrepancy between the zeal with which the Board exposed technical limitations of public interest group witnesses and the way in which assumptions about whose rights would be recognized, how costs and benefits would be distributed, and whose way of life would be protected were not treated as matters for serious public debate. As we will see in the following chapters, these questions were taken more seriously by Berger and his staff, even though in the context of that inquiry more emphasis continued to be placed on assessing consequences than on debates about competing rights and conflicting ways of life.

Notes

1. Quoted by Ann Benedek, "Project North Urges Delay in Development," *The Canadian Churchman*, July/August 1976, p. 11.
2. J.R. Warner, "Letterbasket," *The Canadian Churchman* July/August, 1976.
3. Jon Ferry, "N.W.T. Council Session Ends on Soothing Note," *The Edmonton Journal*, 24 May 1977. This clipping and many of the clippings referred to throughout the study are conveniently available in the publication, *Press Reaction to the Berger Report: A Collection of Clippings from Canadian Newspapers, May 9-June 30, 1977*, compiled by Merv Hey and Leona Olfert for the Institute for Northern Studies at the University of Saskatchewan in Saskatoon.
4. Project North, "A Call for a Moratorium: Some Moral and Ethical Considerations Relating to the MacKenzie Valley Pipeline," reprinted in *Canadian Churches and Social Justice*, ed. John R. Williams (Toronto: Anglican Book Centre and James Lorimer, 1984), p. 164.
5. Ibid., p. 164.
6. Ibid., p. 165.
7. Ibid., p. 165.
8. Cited in François Bregha, *Bob Blair's Pipeline: The Business and Politics of Northern Energy Development Projects* (Toronto: James Lorimer, 1979), p. 67.
9. National Energy Board, *Reasons for Decision: Northern Pipelines*, vol. 1 (Ottawa: Supply and Services Canada, June 1977), pp. 1-57 to 1-65.
10. Ibid., p. 1-61.
11. Ibid., pp. 1-64 to 1-65.
12. Ibid., p. 1-65.
13. Ibid., p. 1-67.
14. Ibid., p. 1-68.
15. Bregha, *Bob Blair's Pipeline*, p. 102.

16. NEB, vol. 1, p. 1-66.
17. Ibid., pp. 1-66.
18. Ibid., pp. 1-80.
19. Ibid., pp. 2-97.
20. Ibid., pp. 2-102.
21. Ibid., pp. 1-71.
22. Ibid., pp. 1-80.
23. Ibid., pp. 1-78.
24. Ibid., pp. 1-84.
25. Ibid., pp. 1-83.

Chapter 4

Assessing the Consequences

In this chapter, attention is shifted from whether the pipeline was needed to its likely impact on native communities, and from the National Energy Board to the Berger Inquiry. Although I will continue to stress the interaction between factual claims and value judgments, I will deal more explicitly in this chapter and the following chapter with the ethical dimension of the debate. Berger's dogged attempts to get to the bottom of the debate over the contribution of hunting, fishing and trapping to the economic life of native communities involved a constant return to the evidence (factual clarification). However, this quest for the truth about economic conditions in native communities, and about the impact of the pipeline, took place in a larger context shaped by certain assumptions about ethical judgments, rational public discourse and the role of public inquiries.

As an initial guess it can be suggested that Berger's mandate and approach reflected a consequentialist or utilitarian understanding of moral judgments and ethical arguments.[1] Making a judgment about the pipeline involved assessing the consequences of proceeding or failing to proceed with construction. To know what the consequences would be for the natives living along the proposed route it would be necessary to have an accurate picture of existing economic conditions in the native communities. However, the initial information provided by industry studies was very different from the information Berger received from the natives themselves and their experts. His attempts to get at the truth about the contribution of hunting, fishing and trapping to the native economy, and to decide what bearing that had on the question of the pipeline, makes a good case study within a case study. The way Berger and the expert witnesses on both sides of the debate combined rigorous empirical inquiry, a pluralistic outlook and the realization that finally a decision about the pipeline would involve an act of human judgment has interesting affinities with the approach to comparative ethics which informs this study. Although I will return more explicitly to that claim in the conclusion, I will begin to clarify it in this chapter by first looking at Berger's mandate and approach; and, second, by examining the conflicting claims and counter-claims about economic conditions in native communities.

73

1. Berger's Mandate and Approach

The federal government appointed Berger to inquire into the economic, social and environmental impact of the pipeline; and to outline the terms and conditions which should be met by the successful applicant. There has been considerable debate over what the federal government intended, and over the way in which Berger interpreted his mandate. Arctic Gas, not surprisingly, assumed that he should stay within narrow boundaries and limit his attention to the terms and conditions for a right of way for the pipeline the federal government had already decided to approve. As a critic of the government's eagerness to build the pipeline to please the United States, François Bregha also maintained that Berger's mandate was in fact confined to a consideration of terms and conditions.[2] Berger himself adopted a broader understanding of the scope of his task. He felt that he was entitled to make judgments about whether or not the pipeline ought to be built, as well as to give advice about terms and conditions.

As Robert Page has pointed out, in order to understand the dynamics of the Berger Inquiry it is necessary to know something about the man. In his intellectual development Berger had been deeply influenced by F.R. Scott, the Montreal civil rights and constitutional lawyer, law professor, poet, and founding member of the democratic socialist League for Social Reconstruction and Co-operative Commonwealth Federation. "Scott above all had articulated the problems facing minorities and dissenters within the Canadian body politic from the point of view of a civil libertarian, a social democrat, and a federal centralist."[3] Berger's record as leader of the British Columbia New Democratic Party (which had replaced the CCF in 1961), and as lawyer for the Nishga Indians of British Columbia, clearly revealed his sympathies with minorities, and in particular with native peoples. He was convinced that what the Canadian majority really stands for will be disclosed in its treatment of marginalized minorities such as native peoples.[4]

Berger also acknowledged the influence of Justices Ivan Rand and Emmett Hall on his understanding of the role of public inquiries. Just as new levels of public thinking about labour relations and health care had emerged from their commissions, perhaps a full and open inquiry into the impact of a northern pipeline could generate new thoughts about northern development and the future of the North. Page has neatly summarized Berger's view that public inquiries had important roles to play, not as substitutes for the political process, but as contributors to a more open and participatory type of politics:

Commissioners of inquiry have an advantage that ministers and senior public servants do not enjoy. They can go out to the people "to hear all the evidence, to reflect on it, to weigh it, and to make a judgment on it." Under cross-examination conflicting viewpoints can be assessed and the evidence weighed. Parliament is supreme, but it requires good advice. In this sense, an inquiry was both an extension of the political process and a catalyst to promote the necessary changes in public opinion, which in turn would bring pressure to bear on those who have appointed the inquiry.[5]

An initial grasp of the nature of Berger's approach can be obtained by considering diametrically opposed responses to what he attempted to accomplish. From the standpoint of University of Saskatchewan economists, J.C. Stabler and M.R. Olfert, Berger was too moralistic and insufficiently rigorous in his determination of the consequences of building or failing to build the pipeline. They complained that the Berger report, "very effectively and emotionally presented pipeline construction up the Mackenzie Valley (within ten years) as an absolute evil against which no protection would be sufficient and for which no adequate compensation could be made."[6] They accused Berger of basing his conclusions on sentimentality:

Overwhelming evidence that the "closed" economy of yore has long since been replaced by vital linkages to the industrial system of the south and that population growth has vastly outstripped growth in the productive capacity of fish, fur and game, is ignored. . . . Instead, nostalgic remembrances, beliefs, fears, hopes, and dreams are taken as "evidence" that hunting, fishing, and trapping are the most important bases of the native economy.[7]

Some of the defenders of a moratorium, on the other hand, expressed their position in terms that made Berger's preoccupation with detailed calculations of the consequences of pipeline construction appear unnecessary, since the Inquiry itself was irrelevant. In his April 26, 1976, presentation, Hugh McCullum stated that even though many of the massive projects already under way in different areas were in legal doubt, they seem to roll on inexorably. "The moral and ethical questions that public interest and native groups attempted to raise were quickly dismissed with this 'greater public good' argument."[8] During cross-examination, the Arctic Gas lawyer asked what Berger's role was if the government had already decided to build the pipeline.

McCullum's response was that Berger did not have a role, since the government was not bound by his recommendations. In response to the lawyer's claim that McCullum was being irresponsible and that the Commissioner should insist that he should be more responsible, Berger indicated that he did not draw as fine a line between the formal hearings and the community hearings as the lawyer might have done. He said that he had decided to follow the path of least resistance, and to let people speak who had things they wanted to get off their chests. That was what hundreds of witnesses in the communities had done, and that was what he had allowed Mr. McCullum to do. He wanted it clearly understood, however, that he rejected "that kind of suggestion that the die is cast, that the Inquiry has no useful function."[9]

Whereas Stabler and Olfert reduced Berger's judgments to sentimental pleading for a long-gone native way of life, those who called for a moratorium implied that further studies were not needed to prove that building the pipeline would be a costly, unjust mistake. The case against the pipeline was already perfectly clear for anyone who was prepared to take seriously the rights of native peoples, and who could see the injustices inherent in the colonial pattern of development which the pipeline proposal represented.[10] Berger remained steadfast in his conviction that it was important to proceed with the task of assessing the likely impact of the pipeline. In order to do this adequately all voices should be heard, and all evidence must be weighed. How native peoples and citizens' groups could make their voices heard in a debate in which one side had already spent over $100 million on complex technical studies was a question Berger took very seriously. The most tangible evidence of this concern was his decision to provide intervener funding for native organizations and public interest groups, to hold community hearings, and to arrange financial support for an alternative group of experts to help native organizations and environmental groups to assess the technical studies presented in support of the Arctic Gas proposal.

Berger believed that his Inquiry could not complete its task unless the various interests which deserved to be heard had the means to prepare and present their cases. Therefore, he arranged for federal government funding for native organizations, environmental groups, northern municipalities and northern business. Berger pointed out that, "These groups are sometimes called public interest groups. They represent identifiable interests that should not be ignored, that, indeed, it is essential should be considered. They do not represent the public interest, but it is in the public interest that they be heard."[11] According to Page, "Berger supplied the native, environmental, municipal and northern business organizations with about $1.8 million, or about 1 per cent of the funds available to Arctic Gas."[12]

During the preliminary hearings native representatives also stressed the importance of Berger hearing directly from native persons themselves. Georges Erasmus, Director of Community Development for the Indian Brotherhood, urged Berger to hold hearings in the communities which would not follow "formal, legalistic procedures."[13] Since the main justification for the pipeline was to meet the energy needs of southern Canadians, the churches in particular urged Berger to hold informal hearings in the South. Berger accepted both suggestions. He held community hearings in ten southern cities as well as in the thirty-five communities in the Mackenzie Valley.

Native organizations and public interest groups faced an additional problem. It would be an immense task requiring high levels of expertise to read and to assess the significance of the millions of dollars worth of technical studies submitted by Arctic Gas in support of its application.[14] A group of experts called the Pipeline Application Assessment Group had been assembled by the federal government to carry out a preliminary assessment of the Arctic Gas application. The summaries and analyses of this group would be available to all participants. In his opening statement to the preliminary hearings, the Arctic Gas lawyer urged Berger not to duplicate the work of the Pipeline Application Assessment Group. He insisted that formal hearings could begin as soon as that group's report was received. Spokespersons for the Canadian Arctic Resources Committee disagreed. They argued that the Assessment Group's interpretation of the Arctic Gas application and its supporting documentation would represent just one opinion. Since, they argued, "there are many, many areas of opinion in assessing environmental and socio-economic data" it would be unfortunate if the only opinion listened to by the Inquiry was the applicant's and the government's. Since impact assessment was a relatively new field of study, "Even the framework of that kind of study is something that we're going to have to enquire about."[15]

In response to the claim that the Pipeline Application Assessment Group's findings would be available for adaptation by any other group, the Canadian Arctic Resources Committee reminded Berger that "the question of assessment is a question of interpretation."[16] Native organizations and environmentalist groups would want to interpret the data used to support the Arctic Gas application from their own perspective. Berger agreed that Arctic Gas and the government had an interest in building the pipeline, and would therefore see the issue from that standpoint. It made sense to fund an alternative group which had a particular interest in protecting the environment. Thus, the Northern Assessment Group, under the direction of the Canadian Arctic Resources Committee, was funded on the understanding that it would provide technical and scientific expertise to assist native organizations and environmentalist groups in their attempts to assess the Arctic Gas application. The work of these countervailing experts added weight to the claims of native peoples that the environmental impact of the pipeline would be far more serious than industry-sponsored studies had predicted.[17]

Berger realized that, as far as the native people were concerned, if he wanted to know about the extent to which they continued to rely upon and to value hunting, fishing and trapping for subsistence use and for exchange within communities he should ask them. The natives wondered why he was listening to those who seek "to quantify, assess their life, their lifestyle, their aspirations as if we were cataloguing something that could be catalogued."[18] Nevertheless, he took seriously the contributions of the social scientists. Their findings must be taken into account along with all of the other voices which must be heard before a judgment could be made about the pipeline. As Berger said:

> If you are going to assess impact properly, you have to weigh a whole series of matters, some tangible, some intangible. But in the end, no matter how many experts there may be, no matter how many pages of computer printouts may have been assembled, there is the ineluctable necessity of bringing human judgment to bear on the main issues. Indeed, when the main issue cuts across a range of questions, spanning the physical and social sciences, the only way to come to grips with it and to resolve it is by the exercise of human judgment.[19]

As a way to illustrate Berger's approach, and to analyse in some detail one aspect of the debate over the pipeline, I will examine the debate about economic conditions in native communities which took place between Charles Hobart, a University of Alberta sociologist, and Michael Asch, an anthropologist from the same university. Their exchanges are particularly interesting from the standpoint of this study.[20] On the one hand, persistent efforts to return to the facts did produce a level of agreement between them regarding precisely defined factual questions that did not appear to be present in their earlier submissions. When claims made by one side were brought into a direct engagement with the counter-claims made by the other side, some disagreements turned out to be misunderstandings, while others were related to differences in the way terms were defined or values were assigned. On the other hand, however, their exchanges indicate how their findings were affected by their basic assumptions about the rationality or legitimacy of their sponsor's projects or aims, and by their interpretative frameworks and social scientific models.

Looking back on the lengthy sessions with each scientist, it is tempting to suggest that it would have been more efficient to deal more directly with their personal stories, and with the nature of their interpretative frameworks and social scientific models. However, there was wisdom in Berger's steadfast refusal to allow attention to be shifted away from concrete questions about the facts. On the one hand, he was proceeding within the framework of a consequentialist approach to moral issues and ethical justification. On the other hand, as I will explain more fully in the final chapter, he was reflecting his training as a trial lawyer and a judge. His approach was in continuity with a casuistical method of practical moral reasoning which starts with concrete cases, takes into account the role of circumstances and the diversity of opinions regarding how specific instances should be evaluated, and assumes that finally human judgment will have to be exercised.

2. The Debate Over Economic Conditions in Native Communities

At one level (i.e., the level of factual clarification) the debate over the contribution of hunting, fishing and trapping to the economies of native communities involved straightforward disagreements about such facts as the number of persons making a living trapping and the value of country food. Before plunging into an analysis of these conflicting factual claims it is helpful to step back and to notice how the different scholars defined the problem.

Both Asch and Hobart were very clear about their definitions of the problem. Because I tend to be more sympathetic to Asch's position than to Hobart's, I must be particularly careful not to recast Hobart's views in a way that makes them seem obviously wrong-headed. Asch placed his arguments in the context of a summary of the industry position: (1) native communities in the North were characterized by high unemployment, high welfare rates, alcoholism, poor housing and racial tensions; (2) these problems cannot be solved through traditional efforts to live off the land because the traditional way of life is dead or dying; and, (3) the pipeline and related activities would provide employment, therefore it would be beneficial, therefore it should be built as soon as possible. His definition of the problem was that the industry proposals would exacerbate rather than alleviate the social problems, and a pipeline would not solve the problem of economic viability for native communities. Thus, his aim was to provide an alternative analysis which would support a different conclusion.[21]

Hobart had a different starting point and a different definition of the problem. He had been asked by Arctic Gas to address a number of questions. For example, he was asked to comment on the validity of the argument that "the provision of stable employment opportunities should be considered a high or top priority, and that the alleviation of poverty would have a positive effect regarding anti-social behaviour."[22] Hobart accepted the validity of both arguments, and was therefore prepared to contradict Asch's negative assessment of the employment provided by the pipeline. Hobart observed that as an anthropologist Asch focused on the persistence of traditional institutions and values while as a sociologist he, Hobart, concentrated on contemporary society and contemporary adaptations. He was particularly concerned about the need to adapt to the hard facts that young people had abandoned traditional skills and that the land was no longer able to support the rapidly expanding native population.[23]

In order to clarify areas of agreement and disagreement, it was necessary to see that the claims made by one side were clearly lined up against the counter-claims made by the other side. There seemed to be strong disagreement about the number of persons making a living as trappers and about the value of country food. A study carried out by Gemini North for Arctic Gas estimated that in 1972 "only 96 persons, out of a study region population of 23,600 and a male working age population of 7,830, were engaged in full-time and regular part-time trapping."[24] The Land Use and Occupancy Study carried out by the Indian Brotherhood of the Northwest Territories reported that 1075 persons rather than ninety-six were actively engaged in trapping in the Mackenzie District.[25] The maps prepared by the Brotherhood depicted a web of interlocking traplines that would be seriously disrupted by a pipeline. This picture of a populated, well-used land was in sharp contrast to the applicant's emphasis on vast empty spaces. It is interesting to notice in passing that the industry's favourite image of the pipeline was that it would be like running a thread across a football field. For native peoples and environmentalists it would be like a knife-slash across the Mona Lisa.

What became clear through cross-examination was that how trappers were counted depended upon whose definition of a trapper was used. As Berger concluded in his report:

> To Gemini North, and to most white people, trapping is
> a job much the same as any other job. So, determining
> the number of trappers is simply a matter of counting
> how many people during the period of the survey ran a

trap line and sold furs. The native people, however, do not see trapping as a job; it is, rather, a way of life based on the use of the land and its resources: running a trap line is but one of a number of seasonal activities. A trapper is, therefore, someone who sees himself as following that way of life. A man who is working for wages with a seismic exploration crew (and who would, therefore, enter Gemini North's figures as a wage employee) might still regard himself as a trapper (or hunter) because he intends to use part of his wages to buy a new snowmobile, a new boat, new traps or a new rifle. In his own eyes, therefore, he is working at "a job" to support "his way of life" as a trapper.[26]

Berger suggested that "statistics on the number of 'trappers,' however they are defined, are not the best evidence of the extent to which the native people still live off the land." He believed that it would make more sense:

to look at the evidence of their actual use of the land today: whether they are engaged in hunting and fishing for subsistence, or trapping for fur, or both. We can understand the native people's vehement rejection of the contention advanced by Arctic Gas that very few of them are trappers only if we appreciate the persistence of their way of life on the land and the persistence of their values associated with the land.[27]

Initial estimates of the value of country food ranged from Gemini North's low figure of five percent to as high as 35 per cent in studies presented as evidence for the native organizations. These disagreements were also related to different judgments about what to include and how to assign measurable quantities to food gathered from the land. For example, the initial Gemini North study on which Hobart had relied had counted only the value of the food sold for cash. The value of the food consumed by the hunters and their families had not been included. There was also a problem with the way value was assigned to food sold. Berger concluded that:

Gemini North attributed to country food only a "local exchange" value, that is, the price that one person would charge another for a commodity, say caribou, within a native community. This method of calculation ignores the fact that the distribution and exchange of country food takes place within the context of kinship obligations and family ties; it is nothing like an ordinary market transaction. So, if we are to understand the real economic value of country food, a standard other than "local exchange" must be used. It is clear from the evidence that the standard that should be applied is the "replacement" value, that is, the amount it would cost a native person to buy from the local store the imported equivalent of the country food he now obtains from the bush and the barrens. It must be plain to anyone that if native people did not or could not obtain country food, they would have to buy meat and fish from the store to replace the food they get now from the land.[28]

Hobart agreed during cross-examination that industry-sponsored studies, including his own, had overstated the belief that the traditional sector of the native economy was dead. He admitted that he was counteracting what seemed to be a tendency on the part of Asch and the others to exaggerate the viability of traditional communities and to underestimate the need for jobs in the other sector of the economy. Asch, on the other hand, had been trying "to provide a balanced view of wage employment in an attempt to counteract the uncritical and enthusiastic way in which the industry sponsored studies have viewed wage labour."[29] By the time the hearings were over Hobart and Asch were more or less in agreement that hunting, fishing and trapping were contributing about 22 per cent to the economies of the native communities in the Mackenzie Valley. That did not mean, however, that they had reached agreement in their judgments about the pipeline.

As Gibson Winter pointed out in his important work, *Elements for a Social Ethic*, social ethics stands at the intersection between social science, which is a retrospective, empirical mode of inquiry, and social policy, which makes future-oriented, normative judgments about what ought to be done.[30] Where the debate between Hobart and Asch becomes really interesting is the point at which they apply their findings to their conclusions about the pipeline. To see how this happened it is helpful to shift attention from reading them horizontally in order to line up their claims and counterclaims to an examination of the vertical connections among the various levels of each position. How did they link their definitions of the problem and their empirical findings to value judgments and conclusions about the pipeline?

3. From Social Science to Social Policy

Hobart drew clear links between the fact that a large percentage of the natives born since 1955 had been socialized away from traditional land-based pursuits; that many of them were unemployed and marginalized; that such marginalization had produced "reactions, responses, and adaptation in native peoples' modes of action which constitute something analogous to the subculture of poverty"; and his predictions of a future without the pipeline. "Thus frustration, bitterness, increased welfarism, despondency and demoralization, increased alcoholism and family breakdown, as Dr. [Mel] Watkins suggested, and certainly increased violence as well, would occur as the opportunities which natives had been trained for and encouraged to anticipate faded away."[31] Problems would no doubt accompany construction of a pipeline, but even more serious problems could be expected without it.

In his attempt to clarify the differences between Hobart and Asch, commission counsel Ian Scott suggested that the two scholars had described as well as they could conditions existing at a particular point in time, and had then attempted to predict the future on the basis of that knowledge. For Hobart, the employment provided by the pipeline would enable natives to recover the pride missing in the previous decade when Hobart's data had been collected. Scott asked whether in his predictions for the future Hobart had taken into account developments in the 1970s which had produced "a more prideful sense of native identity, a new sense of purpose, and a determination to achieve goals which they had set." He wondered whether or not that renewed sense of identity might "fundamentally alter one's ability to predict the future."[32] Hobart replied that he "wouldn't have said that he was predicting the future." What he had been talking about "was the past and the present and I have been talking about what seems to me to be the best course of action." He then caught himself and said that he was not even talking about that. "I have been pointing to needs which I feel must be dealt with—employment needs most importantly in the immediate and the longer range future." That natives now want more input into the decisions affecting their lives, and that they might have a different understanding of who they are as they attempt to meet the problems of their communities, "does not contradict or eliminate certain basic economic realities." Nor does native participation in decisions change one of the most basic facts to which they must adapt, "the carrying power of the land."[33]

Asch's first task was to counteract the industry argument that the traditional sector was dead. He accomplished this goal insofar as

Hobart himself modified his original view and agreed that hunting, fishing and trapping contributed about twenty-two per cent to the native economy. On the precisely defined question about the contribution of country food to the native economy, agreement was reached, and Berger was not forced to take sides. There still remained, however, the question of where the other seventy-eight per cent would come from. Hobart assumed that pipeline construction could be handled in such a way that choices could be freely made whether to stay on the land, to work for wages or to enjoy a combination of the two. Another important part of Asch's argument was that choices were not free, and that the pipeline would not likely provide the kind of employment that would ensure even short-term, to say nothing of long-term, economic or social benefits for the native communities. On the one hand, he had particular concerns such as that most of the jobs would go to young, single males. The money would be spent on luxury items for the employed males rather than on support for families in the communities. On the other hand, his main aim was to reframe the question of economic conditions in native communities and to redefine the problem. Rather than speculating about whether individual natives preferred to hunt and trap or to find employment in the oil and gas industry, he shifted attention to the underlying economic forces which determined the options actually experienced by natives, and he drew attention to the relationship between Hobart's conclusions about the benefits of a pipeline and his taken-for-granted acceptance of an acculturation model.

In response to Hobart's claim that Asch thought that natives preferred trapping to wage employment, and that wage employment was pernicious, Asch insisted that he never argued that natives "preferred" trapping to making cash. "Rather, the point I make repeatedly is that the choices the Dene make regarding the means by which they obtain cash income are not made in a vacuum, but must rather be seen in the context of general social and economic conditions."[34] The decline in full-time hunting and trapping does not necessarily represent voluntary or preferred choices on the part of the Dene as implied in the Gemini North studies. This option was exercised in response to other factors such as the collapse of the fur trade, the location of schools away from bush collection centres and the introduction of an educational system based upon non-traditional values and skills. In a situation characterized by low fur prices and high trade goods prices, there were strong incentives to move into wage employment. If fur prices had been supported [with even a small percentage of the economic supports and incentives enjoyed by corporations in the oil, gas and mining industries], the trend towards wage employment could have been reversed.[35] The problem, according to Asch, was not the inability of natives to make a living off the land, but their loss of control over their lives. Hobart and the other industry representatives aggravated this problem by simply assuming that it was inevitable that native peoples would be assimilated into the mainstream of Canadian life.

Hobart's view was that he was simply reporting what had already happened. He shared Asch's unhappiness with the drift away from the traditional way of life, but he did not think that it was appropriate for a white person to tell natives what they ought to do.[36] Ash maintained, however, that Hobart's conviction that assimilation was already well-advanced, and that further acculturation was inevitable, was deeply influenced by the acculturation model he simply took for granted. Like the earlier generation of western social scientists who developed the acculturation model in connection with their studies of modernization and westernization, Hobart continued to assume that in encounters between technologically advanced and less powerful peoples the weaker group will always adapt to the dominant group. Furthermore, this model assumes "that merely because native people have adopted certain items of western technology, they are losing their traditional values and replacing them with western ones."[37]

Asch shifted attention from the plight of native peoples as passive victims of historical forces beyond their control to their role as agents shaping their future and working out their own patterns of adaptation in a changing world. The solution, according to Asch, was the one proposed by the Dene themselves:

> It is a land settlement, which, if it follows the principles
> laid out in the Dene Declaration, will enable the people
> to regain control over their economic, social, political,
> and all other aspects of their lives. From where they live
> to the education of their young which we control now.
>
> It is this solution which is in full agreement with
> my research findings.[38]

As Scott pointed out during cross-examination, Asch seemed to shift from one type of moral discourse to another when he emphasized the Dene right to control their lives. After a lengthy attempt to determine exactly what features of Dene life would have to remain in order to conclude that traditional ways had been protected, Scott asked whether a Dene-run territories might be an entrepreneurial society like a white Alberta. When Asch said yes, Scott replied: "If that is so, what we are talking about is self-determination and not the restoration of indigenous social structures."[39] Asch reminded him that the only reason so much time had been spent proving the continuing vitality of traditional structures was to counteract the industry claim that the traditional ways were dead. As far as Asch was concerned he had remained within a rigorous consequentialist framework. The consequences of building the pipeline would have damaging effects on the Dene capacity to meet their pressing economic and social needs and to develop the type of economic, social and political structures required for long-term economic well-being.

Asch's belief that the Dene demand for self-determination was rational and his conviction that they had a right to control their own affairs were important parts of his total position. These beliefs and value judgments were not, however, cited as an alternative foundation for his judgment that the pipeline should not be built. His judgment about the pipeline was made concretely and contextually. His findings could have indicated that the pipeline would have a beneficial impact upon the native communities. That would have produced a new situation, and it would have affected both Asch's and the Dene's attitudes towards the pipeline.

Just as Asch appeared to move the discussion beyond consequentialist language to the language of rights and self-determination, he also appeared to push the discussion in an ideological direction by insisting that the underlying economic structures of a capitalist mode of production must be critiqued. Once again, however, he did not shift attention from concrete conditions and empirical findings to abstract debates about conflicting ideologies. In this he and Hobart and Berger were in solid agreement. This respect for mutually accepted procedures of inquiry and argument explains how they were able to sustain the lengthy exchanges that more right-wing scientists like Stabler thought were useless and more left-wing social activists such as the authors of *Moratorium* thought were unnecessary.

In this chapter I have focused once again on the interactions among description, interpretation and evaluation. The amount of time and effort spent attempting to reach agreement about the value of country food illustrated Berger's reliance upon empirically validated evidence. Within the framework of a consequentialist emphasis on judging the rightness or wrongness of a policy by determining its results or consequences, this emphasis on the facts represented one way of dealing with the ethical dimension of the debate in a disciplined, rigorous manner. The question to which I now turn is whether the churches' call for a moratorium before they had access to the evidence gathered during the $5 million, three-and-a-half-year Berger Inquiry represented, as their critics charged, an irresponsible emotional reaction or a different way of assessing the rightness or wrongness of a proposed policy. What I intend to show in the following chapter is that, although the call for a moratorium was rigorously defended within the boundaries of the dominant utilitarian framework, the pro-moratorium position as defended by the native peoples and the churches extended the consequentialist framework in both deontological and ideological directions.

*the science of
duty or moral obligation*   **Notes**

1. A.R.C. Duncan, *Moral Philosophy* (Toronto: CBC Publications, 1965), p. 11: The distinguishing mark of utilitarian theories "is the belief that the rightness and wrongness of human actions is to be explained by reference to their results or consequences, which are judged as good or bad."

2. François Bregha, *Bob Blair's Pipeline: The Business and Politics of Northern Energy Projects* (Toronto: James Lorimer, 1979).

3. Robert Page, *Northern Development: The Canadian Dilemma* (Toronto: McClelland and Stewart, 1986), p. 90. For an excellent cultural study of Scott's life and times, see Sandra Djwa's biography, *The Politics of the Imagination: A Life of F.R. Scott* (Toronto: McClelland and Stewart, 1987).

4. Thomas R. Berger, *Fragile Freedoms: Human Rights and Dissent in Canada* (Toronto and Vancouver: Clarke, Irwin, 1981), p. 247.

5. Page, *Northern Development*, p. 92. The relationship between Berger's understanding of the role of a public inquiry and the tradition of practical moral reasoning called casuistry will be discussed below. For an important new history of this tradition, see Albert R. Jonsen and Stephen Toulmin, *The Abuses of Casuistry: A History of Moral Reasoning* (Berkeley and Los Angeles/London: University of California Press, 1988).

6. J.C. Stabler and M.R. Olfert, "Gaslight Follies: The Political Economy of the Western Arctic," *Canadian Public Policy*, 6 (Spring 1980): 384.

7. Ibid., p. 383.

8. Mackenzie Valley Pipeline Inquiry (MVPI) Transcripts, p. 22233.

9. Ibid., p. 22394.

10. Hugh and Karmel McCullum and John Olthuis, *Moratorium: Justice, Energy, the North, and the Native People* (Toronto: The Anglican Book Centre, 1977), p. 6.

11. Thomas R. Berger, "The Mackenzie Valley Pipeline Inquiry," *Queen's Quarterly* (Spring 1976): 5.

12. Page, *Northern Development*, p. 99.

13. MVPI Transcripts, p. 10.

14. Bregha, *Bob Blair's Pipeline*, p. 41: "The documentation Arctic Gas submitted in support of its project . . . covered some 7000 pages and weighed fifty pounds. Stacked on the floor, it reached the waist of an average-sized person."

15. MVPI Transcripts, p. 58.

16. Ibid., p. 58.

17. The role of the industry-funded Environmental Protection Board should not be forgotten. During the early stages of its preparation of its proposal, Arctic Gas provided 3.5 million dollars to a group of scientists and engineers to study the environmental impact of a Mackenzie Valley pipeline. The group, headed by Carson Templeton of Winnipeg, produced a lengthy report which declared that the present proposal was environmentally unacceptable. For an account of

Berger's appreciation of the role of this group, see his *Queen's Quarterly* article referred to in n. 11.

18. Berger Report, 1, p. 100.
19. Ibid., 1, p. 229.
20. Since my focus in this study has been on the debate within the churches over official church support for the native peoples' call for a moratorium, I have concentrated more on the social justice than on the environmental dimensions of the debate. A further analysis of Berger's handling of conflicting claims regarding environmental impact remains to be carried out. A good starting point would be the differences between the findings of Carson Templeton's Environmental Protection Board and critiques of Berger's conclusions such as L.C. Bliss, "The Report of the Mackenzie Valley Pipeline Inquiry, Volume One: An Environmental Critique," *Musk Ox* 21 (1978): 28-38.
21. MVPI Transcripts, p. 22675.
22. Ibid., p. 25100.
23. Ibid., p. 25101.
24. Berger Report, 1, p. 100.
25. Ibid., p. 100.
26. Ibid., p. 100.
27. Ibid., p. 101.
28. Ibid., p. 101.
29. MVPI Transcripts, p. 24630.
30. Gibson Winter, *Elements for a Social Ethic: Scientific and Ethical Perspectives on Social Process* (New York: Macmillan 1966), pp. 258-64.
31. MVPI Transcripts, p. 25106.
32. Ibid., p. 24219.
33. Ibid., p. 24211.
34. Ibid., p. 24633.
35. Ibid., p. 24633.
36. Ibid., pp. 24131, 25144.
37. Ibid., p. 24639.
38. Ibid., p. 24640.
39. Ibid., p. 24744.

Chapter 5

Competing Rights and Conflicting Ways of Life

The churches had decided to stand openly, officially and wholeheartedly on the side of the natives who opposed the pipeline before the hearings of the National Energy Board or the Berger Inquiry had begun. According to some of their critics this prejudgment was based upon nostalgia for a native way of life which no longer existed, and ignorance about the real needs and desires of natives and non-natives in the North. Church leaders and Project North staff, however, believed that their call for a moratorium was solidly based upon a realistic appraisal of the consequences of northern development schemes, theologically grounded convictions about the rights of natives, and critical judgments regarding the colonial pattern of development and the consumer society values presupposed by the pipeline proposal. In Chapter 4 an examination of conflicting claims about economic conditions in native communities was used to illustrate the dominant consequentialist framework within which the impact of the pipeline was being assessed. In this chapter attention is shifted to the ways in which native leaders and the churches extended the boundaries of that framework by emphasizing other modes of moral reasoning.[1]

The proponents of a moratorium on pipeline construction until native land claims had been settled went beyond the dominant utilitarian or consequentialist framework in two ways. First, their stress on native rights, and their insistence that no major resource development schemes be approved before native claims had been settled, reflected a deontological theory of ethical justification which gets its name from its emphasis on "that which is right."[2] Second, their claim that the pipeline proposal represented a colonial pattern of development, and their demand for the transition to a society based upon conserver rather than consumer values, moved the discussion in an explicitly ideological direction. As I pointed out in the first chapter, I am using ideological in the double sense of pressing the discussion to the level of foundational convictions and of defending judgments about the rightness or wrongness of policies by appealing to a whole way of life.[3] In addition to opening up the dominant consequentialist framework in deontological and ideological directions, the churches explicitly defended both their involvement in the pipeline debate and their particular stance by appealing to Christian teachings and to theological arguments. I will return to that dimension of the debate in Chapter 6.

89

1. The Truth of the Fiction of Group Rights

Compared to "hard facts" about the cost of a caribou roast and the number of natives working as trappers, claims about rights might seem vague and unreal. It should be recalled, however, that decisions about what a caribou roast cost and who was a trapper involved more than positivistic description. Constructing a world in which there were trappers and non-trappers, exchange values and replacement values, involved interpretation, evaluation and invention as well as description. Before trappers could be counted there had to be agreement about whose activities and way of life should be included. The term "trapper," therefore, referred both to a physical reality and a social construction.[4] In an analogous sense, rights claims are social constructions. As Gunnemann has pointed out "the notion of rights rests on a double fiction: the idea of rights itself, and the idea of the individual which it presupposes."[5] In the case of the rights language used by the natives even more ambitious inventions were involved. They were claiming group rights or the rights of collectivities, and they were demanding substantive social rights, such as control of resources, health care and education, as well as formal individual rights such as freedom of speech and freedom of assembly.[6]

I do not want this seemingly flippant reference to rights as fictions, or my introduction of abstract notions about the social construction of reality, to be misunderstood. Although dominant groups tend to take for granted the reality of their own self-definitions, and to see something arbitrary in the attempts of previously silenced majorities or minorities to name themselves and to assert their rights, the claim that our terms and concepts are fictions or social constructions applies to everyone. Even though the aboriginal peoples of the Mackenzie Valley changed the name of their organization from the Indian Brotherhood of the Northwest Territories to the Dene Nation in 1976, this new construct was no more arbitrary than the Canada which had been invented a hundred years earlier. Both of them are historical realities, but both of them are also human inventions in the sense that I am using those terms.

As historical realities, Dene Nation refers to a much older entity than Canada. By the time Abraham was setting out from the land of Ur, the Dene had already occupied their land for 20 000 years. As participants in discussions about the future, the Dene could as plausibly project their hopes for a society based upon co-operation and harmony with nature as the industrial, technological society of southern Canada could cling to its dream of a society characterized by high consumption of non-renewable resources and continuous economic growth.[7] The Dene demand for political control in their homeland involved social constructions, but so did the taken-for-granted assumption that technologically advanced southern Canadians had a right to exploit the resources of "their" last frontier. Industrialized nations act as if there is a divine right of technologically advanced peoples to spread their version of civilization that is analogous to an earlier belief in the divine right of kings. It is important to recall, however, that minority rights can be asserted in a way that implies that majorities do not also have rights. In response to Berger's report, the *Calgary Herald* reminded its readers that: "Sympathy for the rights and aspirations of cultural minorities is essential to a civilized country, but so is a certain hard-headedness about maintaining the rights of the majority."[8]

Although the struggle for aboriginal rights suffered a setback in 1969 when the Trudeau government issued its assimilationist white paper on Indian policy, reactions against that policy and two court cases in 1973 gave the struggle for native rights a great boost. In February 1973 three of seven Supreme Court of Canada judges ruled that the Nishga Indians of British Columbia had aboriginal title to their land which had not been extinguished and which could be asserted today. Three of the judges believed that title had been extinguished, and the seventh judge decided against the case being presented on behalf of the Nishga by their lawyer, Thomas Berger, on technical grounds. He did not pass judgment on the question of aboriginal title. Technically the Nishga had lost, but they had won an important moral victory.[9] Berger was particularly appreciative of the role played by Mr. Justice Emmett Hall.

> Emmett Hall's contributions to Canadian life are numerous. But none is more important than his strong and stirring judgment in the Nishgas' case. For he held that the Nishgas' title could be asserted today. No matter that the province would be faced with innumerable legal tangles. What was right was right.[10]

The second important victory in the courts was Mr. Justice William Morrow's ruling on September 6, 1973, in the Supreme Court of the Northwest Territories that Treaties 8 and 11 had not extinguished aboriginal title to about 400 000 square miles of land in the Northwest Territories.[11] The opposition of the Government of Canada to this ruling, which successfully appealed it in higher courts, forced natives to continue to seek moral and political support for their rights claims which had not yet been secured through the courts. The churches were unexpectedly strong allies in this cultural and political task.

There was lively debate within the churches over how the situation in the North should be defined, and over what followed from the claims that natives owned their land and had a right to participate in the decisions affecting their lives. There was, however, strong official support for the position that native peoples as collectivities did in fact have rights as aboriginal nations which had not been extinguished and rights as human beings which were universalizable. The churches believed that the Government of Canada and the provinces should do what was right and cope with the consequences. This would not only be the right thing to do. It would be better than doing what was politically expedient or in the interests of short-term economic benefits and expecting the natives to cope with the consequences. The willingness of the churches to grant legitimacy to the native peoples' claims to be self-determining nations of aboriginal peoples and to have unextinguished and universalizable rights makes sense in relation to developments which had affected the churches' relations with native peoples.

The early role of the churches in relation to natives was characterized by a lack of respect for native spirituality and culture and a high level of co-operation with the state. Whether or not it was their intention, the churches participated in a process which reduced natives to a condition of powerlessness and dependency.[12] One of the advantages for the churches of the secularization of education and social services in the post-war period was the freedom and incentive it gave them to re-think their relationship to native peoples. In a brief to the Special Joint Committee of the Senate and the House of Commons on March 25, 1947, regarding the Indian Act, the Church of England in Canada expressed the desire to have "our native Canadians . . . advance from segregation and the inferior status of wardship and not remain a backward and inferior minority." Although the Church of England in Canada no doubt had the integration of individuals rather than aboriginal nations in mind, they were convinced that "with adequate guidance and opportunity the Indian people can be advanced to independence and will take a worthy place as citizens of this Dominion."[13]

As Canadian society became increasingly secular and religiously diverse, mainline Protestants, e.g., the Anglican, United and Presbyterian churches, abandoned their earlier assumption that Canada was a Christian society and that they were the dominant religious force. In a post-Christendom Canada they functioned as denominations which no longer dreamed of controlling society, but which refused to withdraw from the public realm and to neglect their continuing sense of responsibility for just and humane public policies.[14] Whereas established churches attempt to control society, and sectarian religious groups withdraw into enclaves of true believers, the feature which characterizes denominations in a religiously diverse society is the desire to transform social structures or to be a transforming presence.[15] The native demands for justice for minorities and ecologically sound energy and resource policies coincided with concerns the churches themselves had been working on with renewed zeal during the sixties.[16]

Another shift in thinking that prepared the formerly mainstream churches to respond positively to the native peoples' desire for more control over their lives was related to changing understandings of mission. The Anglicans once again provide an illustration of new language which provides insights into old as well as new relationships. An item in the May 1976 *Canadian Churchman* recalled "the stir of excitement [which] was felt across the Anglican Communion when a new vision of mission came to birth at the 1963 Congress in Toronto: Mutual Responsibility and Interdependence in the Body of Christ."[17] Even though the mutuality envisioned in 1963 was between First World and Third World Anglican communions, it was a step away from a dominant-subordinate relationship towards a partners-in-mission model. By the early seventies the mainstream Protestant churches and post-Vatican II Roman Catholics were conceiving partnership in more inclusive terms and treating mutuality among equal partners as the criteria for relationships even between donors and recipients of aid.[18]

The most significant influence on the social activist wings of the churches during the late sixties and 1970s was the emergence of liberation theologies in Latin America, Asia and Africa. Within World Council of Churches circles, the Church and Society Conference in Geneva in 1966 was a watershed. For the first time articulate participants from Third World countries out-numbered representatives from Europe, Britain and North America. In the following decade new programs such as the Programme to Combat Racism and the Commission on the Churches' Participation in Development symbolized the shift in focus from a developmentalist approach to Third World poverty to an action-oriented strategy based upon solidarity with liberation movements. Accompanying this growing emphasis on solidarity with oppressed groups was the acceptance of new analyses of the plight of oppressed racial groups and less developed countries. For liberation theologians the problem confronting northern natives and other oppressed groups was not backwardness or underdevelopment, but racism, colonialism and the threat of genocide.

This escalation of the debate through the use of terms such as colonialism and genocide produced conflicting results. On the one hand, it blasted open the boundaries of the dominant, liberal, consequentialist consensus, and provided a more comprehensive framework within which conflicting rights and competing ways of life could be discussed. On the other hand, it introduced a dogmatic basis for bringing the debate to a close. A pipeline which would perpetuate racism and a colonial pattern of development should certainly be opposed. When the stakes were raised in this way, however, it was difficult to sustain an open pluralistic discussion about whether or not colonialism and racism were the most useful terms for describing the North and the plight of Canadian natives. An examination of what was being demanded and what was being resisted will show how difficult it was to keep the claims made by one side and the counter-claims made by the other side clearly aligned with one another as the discussion moved away from specific claims about the pipeline to wider ranging concerns about the rights of natives and the problems of colonialism, consumerism and racism.

2. Aligning Claims and Counter-claims about Native Rights

What was being demanded by the native peoples received eloquent expression in submissions to the Berger and National Energy Board hearings. It was clearly outlined in 1974 by James Wah-Shee, President of the Indian Brotherhood of the Northwest Territories, in an article reprinted by the Social Affairs Department of the Canadian Catholic Conference.[19] He reported a growing awareness on the part of native organizations such as the Indian Brotherhood that "equality is not granted, but must be demanded." In order for native peoples to gain self-respect and a proper role in Canadian society, racial differences could not be ignored. They must be clearly defined and respected. A land settlement based on the formalization rather than the extinguishment of their rights would be "the means by which to define the native community of interest in the North." For such a settlement to have any meaning, the native peoples would require "a resource base under our own control, which ensures our autonomy and our participation as equals in those decisions which affect our lives."[20]

The logic of the native case as Wah-Shee explained it was that: (1) it would not make sense to consider the merits of the pipeline, a particular example of development, apart from an overall development philosophy; (2) regional needs should be included in a development plan; and (3) as part of a region, natives were basing their demand that there be no major development before a land settlement on two grounds: since the rights of native people remain unrecognized by public policy but unextinguished, there should be "no impact assessment *until* these rights have been enshrined"; and "the settlement

. . . itself will be a vital statement of the needs of the region, without which no rational northern development policy can be established." The main problem was that Canada itself had lost control over her resources and thus over her major development decisions. By drifting into a reactive stance regarding development initiatives, Canada was "now being forced to react to a proposal with no regional benefits and questionable national benefits."[21]

The approach to economic development promoted by the natives would attribute "real value to regionally-defined development needs." It would therefore stress regional control rather than compensation for the damage done by projects carried out for the sake of the metropolitan centres. "We are not interested in compensation for the loss of a way of life, but for the right and freedom to construct our own alternatives for development on the bedrock of our past."[22] The twin bases of the native peoples' demand for participation in northern development decisions were, according to Wah-Shee, their ownership of the land and their rights as Canadians. He hoped that the land-use and land-occupancy maps the Indian Brotherhood were working on would help to counteract the rumour that the native people had left the land.[23] As we saw in the previous chapter, the Indian Brotherhood's land-use maps, along with the other testimony of native witnesses at the community hearings and the submissions and arguments of social scientists such as Michael Asch, Scott Rushforth, Peter Usher and Mel Watkins convinced Berger that the native peoples' continuing use of the land was sufficiently significant to justify talking about a dual economy in the North. The question remained, however, of how the control they wished to exercise over their land differed from that of other landowners, such as the southern farmers who had thousands of miles of pipelines running across their lands.

The native peoples' understanding of their right to survive and to continue to occupy the land evolved from an early "land not money" stance to an increasingly political demand for self-determination within the Canadian state. This demand for self-determination was grounded in a universalizable claim about their rights as human beings. The most formal declaration of this stance was passed at the second Joint General Assembly of the Indian Brotherhood of the Northwest Territories and the Métis Association of the NWT on July 19, 1975. It was published as *The Dene Declaration*. Its opening and closing paragraphs stated that: "We the Dene of the N.W.T. insist on the right to be regarded by ourselves and the world as a nation. . . . What we seek . . . is independence and self-determination within the country of Canada. This is what we mean when we call for a just land settlement for the Dene Nation."[24]

Church representatives who supported the Dene Declaration

both helped to convince Berger of the intelligibility and rightness of this stance and worked hard to communicate this position to their southern church constituencies. An effective voice in this regard was Father René Fumoleau, the Oblate priest whose important research on Treaties 8 and 11 had helped to convince Justice William Morrow that the Dene were *"prima facie* owners" of 400 000 square miles of land in the Northwest Territories. He may not have described his contribution in quite these terms, but it can be suggested that he provided the basis for a deontological argument in support of the Dene demand for self-determination and against the pipeline. In one of his addresses in the South, he said:

> The views and aspirations expressed in the Dene Declaration are not isolated in time and space. They are universal because they are part of human nature and of the human spirit. They grow from the very soul of men whom God created in his image and likeness, and to whom he gave intelligence and freedom. The Dene Declaration wasn't born from a desire for a better economic situation, a higher standard of living, better housing, higher wages, larger welfare benefits and a greater opportunity to consume. The Dene, consciously or not, fight for their dignity, for fulfillment, for a more responsible life, for reasons to live, for the right to live their own life in their own way.[25]

The basic stance outlined in this comment by Fumoleau was reiterated in submissions by Dene advisors such as Peter Puxley, Mel Watkins and Gerald Sutton. As aboriginals and as human beings the Dene had unextinguished title to their land and a universalizable right to decide for themselves what constituted their distinctive culture. It was a universalizable claim because being conscious of choices and capable of making them is a central defining condition of being human, and all human groups assert the right to be self-defining and self-determining. Their right to participate in decisions affecting their lives was non-negotiable, and acknowledgement of that right was a prior condition for approving the pipeline. In principle, therefore, until their status as owners of the land was guaranteed, and they were in a position to decide, it would be wrong to build the pipeline.[26]

The Dene demand to control their own lives became more controversial as they became more concrete about the need for separate Dene institutions. In their "Agreement in Principle," prepared for an October 1976 meeting with the Government of Canada, the Dene expressed their lack of trust in non-Dene institutions. Their rights would be protected only through their own "exclusive institutions" which would enable them to "negotiate the terms of all activities affecting our interests long into the future." Anything else, they said, "would be genocide." The need for long-term control was the reason why "recognition, not extinguishment, of rights in the form of an exclusive Dene jurisdiction or government is the first principle of our position."[27]

The Dene insisted that their demand for their own institutions did not mean that they were advocating either separatism or a system of separate development such as the apartheid system in South Africa. They realized that Prime Minister Trudeau was passionately opposed to Quebec separatism, and that any talk about sovereignty would be seen as part of the same threat to Canadian unity that was posed by Francophone demands for independence. Therefore they took great care to affirm that they accepted the sovereignty of the Canadian state. They accepted it reluctantly since, unlike immigrants from other parts of the world, they had not chosen to change their citizenship. The questions of Dene institutions and of the creation of a political entity in which the Dene would be the majority were, however, issues over which there was genuine disagreement as well as misunderstandings about what was being demanded and what was being resisted.

In his presentation to the Berger Inquiry, constitutional expert and University of Toronto political science professor, Peter Russell, argued that what was demanded in the Dene Declaration was consistent with the Canadian constitution. He pointed out that the word "nation" can be used in two ways. It can mean either a group of people united by cultural factors with or without their own territory, or a nation state occupying "a distinct territory and claiming a monopoly of legal control over all who inhabit that territory and legal independence from any external authority."[28] The Dene were a nation in the first sense within the Canadian nation state.

The second aspect of the Dene claim involved the "devolution of decision-making responsibility to Dene institutions of regional and local government." Such a move would require ingenuity on the part of Canadian statecraft, but it would, according to Russell, represent the extension to native peoples of "the liberal philosophy of ethnic partnership" embodied in the original Confederation agreement.[29] If one accepted the principle that the Dene had a right to survive and to develop their own institutions, as well as the factual premise that immediate construction of the pipeline would threaten their survival as a people, then it followed that it would be unjust to build the pipeline until Dene rights had been enshrined and Dene institutions had been developed. This form of the argument against the pipeline combines a deontological emphasis on what is right and a utilitarian assessment of consequences. A pure deontological argument would be that even if the benefits could be shown to outweigh the damages it would be wrong to proceed until Dene rights were enshrined and Dene institutions had been developed. Insofar as the native leaders and the churches demanded a moratorium until claims were settled without carefully balancing the legal and political complexities of such a demand against the damaging impact of the pipeline, their position reflected a deontological mode of moral reasoning. This characterization of their position does not necessarily make their argument more moral or unassailable. It does, however, identify the type of reasoning involved, and establishes the unfairness of assuming that they were simply being emotional and ignoring the hard facts.

One of the persons who disagreed in principle with the Dene demand for separate political institutions was Senator Jack Austin. He had been intimately involved with economic and political developments in the North as executive assistant for the Minister of Northern Affairs and Natural Resources in the 1960s. He believed that it would be wrong in principle to use ethnicity as a factor for determining citizenship, voting rights, eligibility for political office or job advancement. He endorsed the Prime Minister's refusal to negotiate with separatism wherever it may appear in the country while admitting that "our confederation is not cast in iron. It is amenable to amendment, and it is amenable to change in the context of the total benefits which all Canadians wish to have from their roles as citizens of this country."[30] In his view:

> Once you get into ethnicity as a criterion for politics, the world goes backwards. Why shouldn't the Ukrainians have a separate state in Saskatchewan? Why shouldn't the Jews run Winnipeg, the Italians run Toronto? The greatest principle of Western democracy is that each man is equal to each other man and these distinctions don't matter. What matters is fairness, ability and the ability to be mobile in society according to your talents, and not how you're born and what your status was.[31]

Austin agreed, when asked by the interviewer, that he was defending a moderate position in relation to more radical diagnoses of what the native people were up against and more radical prescriptions for the future of the North. His defence of his moderate stance was based in part upon his philosophical conviction that ethnic or racial difference was the wrong basis upon which to organize political institutions. It was also based upon his confidence that the political evolution of the North was advancing towards more local and regional control for northern branches of government, and towards more meaningful participation in those institutions on the part of natives. The natives and their supporters were much more critical of existing arrangements, and much less confident of the direction in which political organizations and economic realities were evolving in the North. Rather than focusing on the evolution of native peoples and northern institutions from one stage to another in a continuous progressive process, they drew attention to co-existing patterns of development which were in conflict with one another.[32]

From the standpoint of the natives and their supporters, the rights demanded by the natives would never become realities unless the problem was properly diagnosed. In their view, what the natives were up against was not simply metropolitan sluggishness in granting representative government to "the last frontier." They were engaged in a struggle against the evils of colonialism, consumerism and racism.

3. Combatting Colonialism, Consumerism and Racism

In his opening statement to the Berger Inquiry preliminary hearings, Glen Bell, lawyer for the Dene, pointed out that the "land not money" position was not simply a negotiable opening bid. It was, he said:

> the formal expression of a more fundamental issue which will be before the Inquiry. The issue is one which involves the struggle between two opposing concepts of economic development for the North. The pipeline proposal represents the "colonial" philosophy of development. Opposed to this notion of northern development is the "community" philosophy of development as exemplified by the native land claim.[33]

Berger acknowledged the existence of different philosophies of development, but he tried to keep the debate focused on the facts which would help him to assess the impact of the pipeline, and on the reasons used by different participants to explain and defend their needs and aspirations. As I will explain in the following chapter, this approach reflected both the nature of his mandate and his own assumptions about practical reasoning and public choices.[34] In their submissions to the Berger Inquiry and the National Energy Board, Project North staff and representatives of the churches both expanded the range of facts which would be relevant for assessing the impact of the pipeline and attempted to move the debate in an explicitly ideological direction.

In their April 27, 1976, presentation to the Berger Inquiry, which was also submitted to the National Energy Board, the Project North staff team graphically described the pattern of development they experienced as they travelled across the North. In order to predict the impact of a Mackenzie Valley pipeline it would be necessary to understand the nature of this pattern and of the ideology which made that approach to economic development appear to be natural and good. Underlying surface differences among major projects, such as the James Bay hydro development in Quebec, the Nelson-Churchill river diversion scheme in Manitoba, and plans for industrial development in northwestern British Columbia, there was a common pattern. The projects were always large; there were massive expenditures of money during the construction phases; workers were usually brought in from the outside; the projects were planned secretly outside the area concerned and announced as if final decisions about them had already been made; they usually involved native lands that were "protected" by the Indian Act or not yet ceded through treaties or land settlements; they were usually socially disruptive and environmentally hazardous; and there were often enormous cost overruns due in part to bad planning and hasty implementation. The McCullums concluded, first, "that the human concerns of the indigenous peoples seeking some form of self-determination are always secondary to the profits of industrial developers." Secondly, when these damaging consequences "are drawn to the attention of governments and corporations and they are forced to acknowledge their mistakes, the response is always that 'in the greater public interest' we have decided to proceed notwithstanding all other problems."[35]

As the lawyers cross-examining the McCullums discovered, it was not easy to take apart the McCullums' position in order to test the accuracy and the implications of particular claims. From the standpoint of persons who did not share their basic description of what was going on in the North, the McCullums' submission sounded more like an ideological denunciation of a whole way of life than an argument based upon carefully documented, measurable consequences. As I have suggested, their aim was to contribute to the debate over the predicted impact of the pipeline by pressing for a broader framework and a more explicit analysis of conflicting philosophies of development and ideologies. As we saw in the earlier introduction to the Project North brief to the Berger Inquiry, the dominant framework was broadened, first, by a critique of the assumptions guiding Canadian public policy-making. A second strategy for broadening the framework in a more explicitly ideological direction involved comparative studies designed to show what had happened to native peoples in other parts of the world when a colonial pattern of resource development had been used.

Regarding the assumptions embedded in the established order, the Project North brief objected to an order characterized by "social and economic patterns of behaviour that bind and oppress, give privilege to the powerful and maintain systems of dependency, paternalism, racism and colonialism." Other assumptions were:

> 1. that our society, as it presently operates, is basically sound, and that, at most, a few adjustments are required to cope with changing conditions;
> 2. that problems can be isolated and analyzed, and that the results can be re-integrated with other factors on the basis of rational, functional calculations.[36]

The problem with these assumptions is that too much emphasis is placed upon continuity with existing practices and the role of "experts" with only a "nod in the direction of citizen participation." The denial of citizen participation would be unjust even if the system was delivering the goods. However, since that is not the case it must be criticized on consequentialist grounds as well. Both the results of previous resource development schemes, and the basic principles in accordance with which they are planned and carried out, are unacceptable from the standpoint of justice and equality. The problem, according to the Project North brief, is that the pipeline proposal represents a further example of profit-seeking corporations, a compliant government, and a wasteful, energy-hungry southern Canada preparing to sacrifice the way of life of northern natives for a few years supply of natural gas. In such a struggle, the churches must be prepared to take sides:

> For there to be equality in this struggle it is necessary for the churches and all other groups interested in the moral and ethical questions of Northern development to stand officially, openly and clearly on the side of justice for and the human rights of the Native People of this country.[37]

The churches believed that knowledge about the fate of native peoples in other parts of the world would help Canadian decision-makers to assess more adequately the likely impact of the pipeline on northern native communities. They decided to compare resource extraction and land clearance schemes in the Amazon Valley of Brazil with the approach taken to massive developments in Canada's far North. In the fall of 1975, shortly after Project North had been created to work with native organizations and to engage in consciousness-raising education with southern churches, another working group, the Corporate Action Research Project (CARP), was created to study the parallels between Brazil and Canada.[38] A brief based upon CARP-sponsored research was presented to the Berger Inquiry on April 26, 1976. Its basic argument was that in order to understand the probable impact of the pipeline, it was "important to examine the struggles of native peoples elsewhere in the world who have encountered similar patterns of resource development." The seventeen pages of evidence in the brief provided convincing support for the claim that the native peoples of the Amazon Basin had been ruthlessly deprived of their land. The provocative part of the brief, of course, involved the comparison between Brazil and Canada.

The main features of the Brazilian situation were that the resource development schemes were "primarily controlled by transnational corporations, receiving the active support of the Brazilian government and serving interests outside of Brazil"; natives had no control over the decisions affecting their land and their lives; and, not only were the natives needs not met, their culture and their way of life were destroyed.

The parallels between Brazil and Canada were that in both cases the areas in question are regarded as resource frontiers; present occupants of the land are threatened; the lack of effective native participation in decision-making is aggravated by the conflict of interest within the government departments which, in Canada as in Brazil, have responsibilities for Indian affairs and northern development; and, in both areas many of the same corporations are there to extract resources for export rather than to serve the interests of local inhabitants.[39]

During cross-examination, representatives from the churches, Oxfam and the Latin American Working Group who had collaborated on the research were pressed to clarify the implications of the findings presented in the brief for a decision about the pipeline. Arctic Gas and Inquiry lawyers wanted to know whether it was being assumed that the Dene should have absolute sovereignty over their land and thus be exempted from expropriation procedures. The lawyers wanted to know what conditions should have been met before development had been allowed to proceed in the Amazon Basin. The main answer they received to these questions was that time was needed, and that, therefore, "there should be a moratorium on all major resource development."[40]

Berger's line of questioning was interesting. Regarding the churches' comments about the energy needs of southern Canadians, he asked whether they were "saying to the people in southern Canada that it may be necessary in order to do what is right by the people of the north for you to curtail your standard of living." The answer was that lifestyles would have to be restrained, but even more important were the changes required in economic and social structures.[41]

The basic convictions that the natives had a right to control their lives, and that the pipeline proposal took it for granted that the powerful could impose their will on the powerless, provided absolute, non-negotiable grounds for attempting to block the pipeline. An additional reason provided by the churches for demanding a moratorium was related to the stewardship of non-renewable resources and to the way of life of southern Canadians. Recent studies such as the Club of Rome's *Limits to Growth*, the churches' involvement in the World Population Conference at Bucharest and the World Food Conference at Rome in May and November of 1974, and the churches' growing concern about environmental issues led to a sense of urgency about human survival. Project North cited as one of its main reasons for pressing for a moratorium on major northern resource development projects the need for time "to give Canadians an opportunity to work together to develop alternative lifestyles, based on conserver rather than consumer attitudes."[42]

In light of the environmental crisis caused by the wasteful, energy-intensive lifestyle of southern Canadians, and the social costs of an economic system based upon competition and greed, it was the natives who were pointing the way to a viable future. As Peter Puxley said in his submission to the Berger Inquiry, the oil companies and the federal government "are the ones to whom the phrase 'You can't go back to your traditional ways' is truly applicable."[43] The churches were calling on southern Canadians to wake up and to realize that "Native People are on the cutting edge of turning the direction of our society's growth from materialism and consumerism to a more fundamentally human concept. In some ways the North is fighting the South's battles."[44]

Since no one explicitly defended the consumer society, the claims and counter-claims at this level of the debate were not very well aligned with one another. Church members who worked in the oil and gas industry were particularly disparaging of the picture of corporations and Canadian life presented in the Project North brief and other church statements. Rather than seeing free-wheeling corporations making huge profits by exploiting unneeded resources for a wasteful South, they saw a highly regulated, conservation-conscious industry attempting to meet the minimal energy needs of all Canadians who live in heated houses and who drive cars or snowmobiles. An Anglican cleric, Canon Randall Ivany, spoke for many of them in his November 18, 1977, address to the Anglican Diocese of Edmonton's "Bishop's Men." He accused church leaders of listening only to left-wing radical voices as a basis for its criticisms of the Mackenzie Valley pipeline, of seeking confrontation rather than reconciliation, and of "alienating the very people who by their work and money keep the church alive." He pointed out that: "A lot of the middle and upper income group are coming to the conclusion that the church hasn't got interest or time for them any more."[45]

The United Church's Northern Co-ordinating Committee related positively to an emphasis on energy stewardship. Members of that committee who disagreed with Project North's call for a moratorium did not see why the two sides could not work together in areas where there was agreement. They supported the right of the native people to a just settlement, but they insisted that there "is not just one north but many and not all native groups favour a moratorium." They saw no reason to tie the energy stewardship aspect of the debate so tightly to the question of a land claim settlement. It should be possible to work together on an alternative energy policy for Canada in spite of disagreements about the legitimacy of blocking development projects until land claims were settled.[46]

Although the problem of racism was always an integral part of the radical diagnosis of what the natives were up against,[47] the churches did not stress racism as a factor in their submissions to the Berger Inquiry or the National Energy Board. Some of the natives talked about genocide, but the language of racism was not a prominent part of the Mackenzie Valley pipeline debate which is the focus of this study. Reactions to the later use of that language are, however, relevant for this study because they provide a further illustration of the double impact of terms such as racism, colonialism and genocide.

On the one hand, as the Project North staff later pointed out regarding the harshness of the early formulations of the natives' demands, there was a need to draw attention to the seriousness of the problem.[48] It was necessary to challenge Canadian complacency about our country, and about the treatment of "our" natives compared to the more obviously racist apartheid system in South Africa and the more blatantly colonial pattern of development in Brazil.[49]

On the other hand, escalation of the debate with the use of densely packed terms which combine description and denunciation make it difficult to keep the discussion going between persons who see the aptness of those terms and those who do not. I will use the reactions of the Anglican Bishop of the Arctic, John Sperry, to grants to northern native groups from the World Council of Churches' Programme to Combat Racism to illustrate this point.

The Project North brief to the Berger Inquiry used Bishop Sperry's impassioned plea for the recognition of native rights at the 1975 Anglican Synod to symbolize the churches new level of commitment to native peoples. The churches, said Bishop Sperry, must be like the Good Samaritan

> who not only bound up the wounds inflicted by a cruel and heartless society that left a race of people to die, but who stood clearly beside this man and continued to support him when all others had abandoned him, and helped him morally and with action.
>
> If we today fail to place ourselves clearly on the side of Native People in Canada, and instead pass by on the other side by refusing to state clearly with words and actions where we stand, then we must return to our homes from this place and hang our heads in shame.[50]

By the time the Canadian churches were drafting their resolutions in support of native rights claims, the World Council of Churches had increased the tempo of its witness against racial discrimination. Before the Programme to Combat Racism had been launched in the late sixties, the WCC tended to talk about inter-racial relations rather than racism. The first event sponsored by the new program, the 1969 Nottinghill Consultation, urged the churches to be prepared, "all else failing," to support "resistance movements, including revolutions, which are aimed at the elimination of political or economic tyranny which makes racism possible."[51] These recommendations were adopted by the Central Committee at its 1969 meeting, and a special fund for the support of groups fighting against racial oppression was established. When grants from this fund were received by native organizations in northern Canada, church leaders in the North such as Bishop Sperry and Reverend Jim Ormiston, the United Church minister at Yellowknife, were outraged. It was one thing to affirm the natives right to a just settlement of their claims. It was a quite different thing to use a term like racism to define the relationship between whites and natives in their communities.

What was particularly controversial about the Programme to Combat Racism grants was that northern native groups qualified for grants from a fund set up to assist groups facing physical or cultural genocide. Top priority for PCR grants was support for groups stuggling against apartheid in South Africa. In the selection of other areas account was taken "of those places where the struggle is most intense and where a grant might make a substantial contribution to the process of liberation; particularly where racial groups are in imminent danger of being physically or culturally exterminated."[52] Insult was added to injury when arrangements for the grants were made without consultation with northern church leaders.

Reactions to the PCR grants both brought into clearer focus tensions that already existed during the debate over the pipeline and illustrated the complexities which characterized the post-Berger phase of the native peoples' struggle for self-determination. Project North's polarizing, confrontational, "prophetic" stance represented a timely response to the life-threatening possibility that a pipeline would be built before the natives' title to their land had been clearly established. Their sense of urgency was justified by the federal government's explicitly defended intention to extinguish rather than to enshrine aboriginal rights. By the end of the 1970s, even though native claims had not been settled, the collapse of the threat of the Mackenzie Valley natural gas pipeline, and the willingness of the Dene to become joint owners of drilling rigs with Esso Resources, had produced a new situation. The impact of these new conditions on the roles of solidarity groups such as Project North, and on the persons responsible for the routine pastoral work of the churches, underlines the importance of understanding the contextual nature of the earlier responses of each group.

My aim in the preceding chapters has been to clarify different dimensions of the pipeline debate and to show how a debate about public choices, which at first glance seemed to pit church leaders against business people, took place within each church as well. When looked at from within each stance there seemed to be an obvious and debate-stopping connection between their attitude towards the pipeline and the biblical or theological foundations of their positions. Project North's call for a moratorium appeared to flow directly from the demands of the prophetic tradition to be in solidarity with the native peoples' cry for justice. Resistance to this confrontational stance was based on the fact that the churches sponsoring Project North included members on both sides of the issue, and on the biblically grounded conviction that Christians should try to make a reconciling rather than a divisive contribution to the debate. My task in the next chapter will be to examine the role played in the debate by appeals to basic convictions and religious teachings. Although some participants in the debate gave the impression that biblical teachings could provide a source of certainty about what ought to be done which could authoritatively resolve the dispute, I will suggest that there are more helpful ways to think about appeals to scripture and tradition. On the one hand, these appeals broadened the framework within which the debate proceeded. On the other hand, they demonstrated the churches' continuing capacity in a secular, pluralistic, modern society to reconnect language about rights, consequences and ways of life to a theologically grounded teleological vision of what is right and good and true.[53]

Notes

1. This chapter continues to focus attention on moralities as languages of persuasion. My immediate concern is to show how the languages of human rights and ideology critique extended the realm of moral discourse beyond the dominant consequentialist framework. I am aware of the possibility that the churches enhanced the persuasive power of these modes of discourse by linking them explicitly to a theologically grounded teleology or view of the human and cosmic good. See Jon Gunnemann, "Human Rights and Modernity: The Truth of the Fiction of Individual Rights," *Journal of Religious Ethics* 16, 1 (Spring 1988): 182.

2. A.R.C. Duncan, *Moral Philosophy* (Toronto: Canadian Broadcasting Corporation, 1965), p. 11.

3. Ibid., p. 11. See also Gibson Winter, *Elements for a Social Ethic: Scientific and Ethical Perspectives on Social Process* (New York: Macmillan, 1966), p. 66: "The peculiar character of ideological formulation is that it selects elements of the cultural heritage and lifts them to a new level as expression of the society's future; in this sense, it has a particularly political character, giving symbolic form to the unity and meaning of the social enterprise."

4. See Peter Berger and Thomas Luckmann, *The Social Construction of Reality* (Garden City, New York: Doubleday, 1966). For a similar perspective, see Dorothy E. Smith, *The Everyday World as Problematic: A Feminist Sociology* (Boston, Mass.: Northeastern University Press, 1987), and *Texts, Facts and Femininity: Exploring the Relations of Ruling* (London and New York: Routledge, 1990).

5. Gunnemann, "Human Rights and Modernity," p. 160.

6. For good discussions of the relationship between individual and social rights, see Patrick Kerans, "The Struggle against Dependency: Equality as Individuals or as Peoples," in *Traditions in Contact and Change*, ed. Peter Slater, Don Wiebe, Maurice Boutin and Harold Coward (Waterloo, Ont.: Wilfrid Laurier University Press, 1983); and David Hollenbach, *Claims in Conflict: Retrieving and Renewing the Catholic Human Rights Tradition* (Toronto and New York: Paulist Press, 1979).

7. Peter Puxley, "The Colonial Experience," in *Dene Nation—The Colony Within*, ed. Mel Watkins (Toronto and Buffalo: University of Toronto Press, 1977), p. 106: "To one involved in the Dene struggle to assert their right to survive, it is quite clear that Canadian society, and the corporations whose imperative defines our choices, are the real 'traditionalists' today. The Dene proclaim a new future, while the oil companies and the federal government keep turning to the past. They are the ones to whom the phrase 'You cannot go back to your traditional ways' is truly applicable."

8. *Calgary Herald*, 11 May 1977, p. 53.

9. François Bregha, *Bob Blair's Pipeline: The Business and Politics of Northern Energy Development Projects* (Toronto: James Lorimer, 1979), p. 31. See also Sally Weaver, *Making Canadian Indian Policy: The Hidden Agenda 1968-70* (Toronto: University of Toronto Press, 1981).

10. Thomas R. Berger, *Fragile Freedoms: Human Rights and Dissent in Canada* (Toronto and Vancouver: Clarke, Irwin, 1981), p. 274.

11. René Fumoleau, OMI, *As Long As This Land Shall Last: A History of Treaty 8 and Treaty 11, 1870-1939* (Toronto: McClelland and Stewart, 1973), p. 13.
12. John Badertscher, "Irony and Liberation: A Study in Canadian History," *The Annual of the Society of Christian Ethics: 1982* (Waterloo, Ont.: Council on the Study of Religion, 1982), pp. 45-70.
13. Brief by the Church of England in Canada to the Special Joint Committee of the Senate and the House of Commons regarding the Indian Act, 25 March 1947, p. 1.
14. See John Webster Grant, "Religion and the Quest for a National Identity: The Background in Canadian History," in *Religion and Culture in Canada/Religion et Culture au Canada*, ed. Peter Slater (Corporation Canadienne des Sciences Religieuses/Canadian Corporation for Studies in Religion, 1977), pp. 7-22; and Anthony Battaglia, "Sect or Denomination: The Place of Religious Ethics in a Post-Churchly Culture," *The Journal of Religious Ethics* 16, 1 (Spring 1988): 128-42.
15. This basic stance was clearly articulated in the United Church's "Report of the Commission on Christianizing the Social Order," *Record of Proceedings, Sixth General Council, Kingston, Ontario, 1934*. For more recent uses of the transformationist image, see the Canadian Conference of Catholic Bishops' "A Society to be Transformed," December 1977 in Do Justice! The Social Teaching of the Canadian Catholic Bishops, ed. E.F. Sheridan, S.J. (Sherbrooke and Toronto: Éditions Paulines and the Jesuit Centre for Social Faith and Justice, 1987), pp. 326-34; the Anglican Church's 1977 paper, "A Transforming Influence: Native Peoples and Northern Development, Social Justice and the Church"; as well as H. Richard Niebuhr's classic *Christ and Culture* (New York: Harper & Brothers, 1951).
16. John R. Williams, ed., *Canadian Churches and Social Justice* (Toronto: Anglican Book Centre and James Lorimer, 1984).
17. Carolyn Purdon, "Third World Voice Urges Mission Partnership," *Canadian Churchman,* December 1974, p. 9.
18. See my "Social Action and Mission in the Eighties," in *Justice As Mission: An Agenda for the Church: Essays in Appreciation of Marjorie and Cyril Powles*, ed. Terry Brown and Christopher Lind (Burlington, ON: Trinity Press, 1985), pp. 85-94.
19. James Wah-Shee, "Model for Indian Claims," in *Social Thought* (Ottawa: Social Action Department of the Canadian Catholic Conference, Fall 1974).
20. Ibid., p. 2.
21. Ibid., pp. 2-3.
22. Ibid., p. 4.
23. Ibid., pp. 4-5.
24. Printed in Watkins, *Dene Nation*, pp. 3-4.
25. René Fumoleau, "Great Spirit and Dene Nation" unpublished address, Toronto, 22 August 1977, p. 7.
26. Watkins, *Dene Nation*, p. xi: The Dene "have come to the fundamental perception that their struggle is for the most universal of human rights, the right to be a self-determining people. It is this right which the Dene insist the federal government must recognize as an integral part of aboriginal rights."
27. Printed in Watkins, *Dene Nation*, p. 183.
28. Peter Russell, "The Dene Nation and Confederation," in Watkins, *Dene Nation*, pp. 165 and 172.

29. Ibid., p. 172. See also, Michael Asch, *Home and Native Land: Aboriginal Rights and the Canadian Constitution* (Toronto: Methuen, 1984).

30. "Senator Austin on Self-Determination," *The Drum*, 18 June 1977, p. 245.

31. "Ethnicity: Dene's Ghetto Spectre," *The Drum*, 18 June 1977, p. 246.

32. This difference in basic orientation reflects the consensus and polarization models of politics discussed by Charles Taylor in *The Pattern of Politics* (Toronto/Montreal: McClelland and Stewart, 1970); and the functionalist-voluntarist debate analysed by Winter in *Elements for a Social Ethic*. See also Malcolm Hector McRury, "Debating the Past and the Future: An Analysis of Conflicting Views of History within the MacKenzie Valley Pipeline Inquiry, 1974-1977," M. Phil. thesis, Toronto, Institute for Christian Studies, n.d., pp. 117-18.

33. MVPI Transcripts, p. 812.

34. Ronald Manzer, "Public Policy-Making as Practical Reasoning," *Canadian Journal of Political Science*, 17, 3 (September 1984): 577-94.

35. MVPI Transcripts, pp. 22230-268. This submission by Hugh McCullum and Karmel Taylor McCullum was based upon the research they had done for their book, *This Land Is Not For Sale* (Toronto: Anglican Book Centre, 1975).

36. Project North, "A Call for a Moratorium," in John R. Williams, *Canadian Churches and Social Justice* (Toronto: Anglican Book Centre and James Lorimer, 1979), pp. 157-58.

37. Ibid., p. 161.

38. The Corporate Action Research Project was staffed by Mary Bird of GATT-Fly and supported by additional funds from the Anglican and Roman Catholic churches. During the winter of 1975-76 Roger Rolf of Oxfam, Larry Pratt of the University of Alberta and the GATT-Fly staff carried out research projects which provided the basis for the April 1976 brief to the Berger Inquiry called "Colonial Patterns of Resource Development."

39. "We Stand On Guard . . . for Whom?: The Corporate Pattern of Resource Development and the MacKenzie Valley Pipeline" (a popularly written summary of CARP's research on Brazil and the Canadian North).

40. MVPI Transcripts, pp. 22168-198.

41. Ibid., p. 22214. In the first volume of his report, Berger acknowledged the need for structural changes, but he drew on an older tradition than the Latin American dependency theory which informed the churches' brief. In his response to a suggestion that he had been influenced by Third World parallels, he pointed out that he relied "on the staples theory of Canadian history as developed by H.A. Innis back in the 1930s and 1940s. You will see that my analysis in Chapter 9 (under the heading "Economic Development of the Northern Economy") is to a great extent a reflection of Innis' work." From a letter quoted by Mathew Zachariah in "The Berger Commission Inquiry and the Revitalization of Indigenous Cultures," *Revue Canadienne d'études du développement/Canadian Journal of Development Studies* 5, 1 (Summer 1984): 70.

42. Project North, "A Call for a Moratorium," in Williams, *Canadian Churches*, p. 156. Two important Science Council of Canada reports from this period were *Population, Technology and Resources* and *The Conserver Society*.

43. Puxley, "The Colonial Experience," in Watkins, *Dene Nation*, p. 106.

44. Project North, "A Call for a Moratorium," in Williams, *Canadian Churches*, p. 161.

45. Tom Harpur, "Businessmen Protest Churches' Social Activism: Arctic Development and Foreign Dealings Spark Controversy," *The Toronto Star*, 26 February 1977, p. F4.

46. Muriel Duncan, "Moratorium: Not Easy to Reach Consensus on Church Stand," *United Church Observer*, January 1977, pp. 34-35. See also the 28 April 1977 minutes of the United Church's Northern Co-ordinating Committee.

47. See the 1976 interview with Karmel and Hugh Mccullum, "That Old Demon Racism," *Vanguard*, November-December 1976, pp. 7-11.

48. See John R. Sperry, Bishop of the Arctic, "Report to the Unit on Public Social Responsibility: Analysis of Project North," 8 January 1980; and 11 February 1980 response by the Project North staff. General Synod Archives.

49. Bishop Sperry could understand the need for the native peoples themselves to dramatize the seriousness of their situation, but he expected the World Council of Churches and the Anglican Church to take a more balanced approach.

50. Project North, "A Call for a Moratorium," in Williams, *Canadian Churches*, p. 158.

51. Ans J. van der Bent, ed., *Breaking Down the Walls: World Council of Churches' Statements and Actions on Racism 1948-1985* (Geneva: World Council of Churches, 1986), p. 10. As part of the close relationship between Project North and the World Council of Churches, the Project North staff did most of the research and writing for "No Last Frontier," *Risk*, 13, 2 (Geneva: World Council of Churches, 1977).

52. Van der Bent, *Breaking Down the Walls*, pp. 77-78.

53. See Gunnemann, "Human Rights and Modernity," p. 182: "The crucial question is how and whether this flowering of rights language under conditions of modern differentiation can be practically and institutionally reconnected or restored to its implicit teleological framework. Such a restoration would entail the development of a differentiated moral language adequate to the differentiated spheres of modern social life, governed by a teleological vision."

Chapter 6

Post-ethical Clarification
and Religious Convictions

The Mackenzie Valley pipeline debate is a particularly relevant case study for persons who are interested both in the ethical and religious dimensions of the debate and in the role of the churches in Canadian society. These two interests converge insofar as the churches were the participants who most vigorously insisted that fundamental ethical and religious issues were at stake. In this chapter I will address more explicitly the distinctive contribution of the churches by examining the appeals to religious convictions and church teachings by participants on both sides of the debate.

1. Religious Convictions and Public Choices

As a creation of the churches, Project North's main mandate for the positions it took came from resolutions adopted by its sponsoring denominations. Thus, in its April 1976 brief to the Berger Inquiry,various church statements were cited as the authority for Project North's intervention.[1] In their September 1975 Labour Day message, the Roman Catholic bishops had urged Catholics and others to act "in solidarity with the Native Peoples of the North in a common search for more creative ways of developing 'the last frontier' of this country." The Anglicans at their 1975 Synod meeting had called for a halt to "planned development until aboriginal claims are settled." The United Church had also passed a resolution "in support of the Indians of Canada making their claims for land." In March 1976 the leaders of Canada's five major denominations and the Canadian Council of Churches met with Prime Minister Trudeau and members of the Cabinet. In a document called *Justice Demands Action* the church leaders asked the federal government to declare a moratorium until native claims had been settled.[2] The Presbyterians, Lutherans and Mennonites later joined Project North on the basis of policies deeply rooted in their own traditions.

The authors of the Project North brief suggested that some people in society "would say that the Church should not be involved in political, economic or social issues." These people argue "that the Church is concerned with man's soul and lacks the expertise to deal adequately with other matters."[3] In its rejection of that view, the brief turned "to the biblical imperatives of justice and liberation for the poor, the dispossessed and the minorities of the world (Habakkuk 2:9-10; Amos 5:7-11)."[4] The churches should be involved in social issues because:

> the Gospel proclaims that God's sovereignty includes all realms of life. Nothing that is human can be outside the Church's mission. It is the love of God in Christ for man that is the basis of the church's social and political concern. In particular, this means that we stand in solidarity with the native peoples of Canada who face the inseparable connection between themselves as a people, and the stewardship of the earth's resources.[5]

The churches should criticize existing arrangements, first, because they are sinful. "By social sin, we mean that we create and sustain social and economic patterns of behaviour that bind and oppress, give privilege to the powerful and maintain systems of dependency, paternalism, racism and colonialism." Second, however, "Christians are called to take a critical stance regarding the social reality of each time and space." The Gospel sheds critical light "on the structures and procedures of our institutions, governments and corporations and calls into question many of the images and norms which prevail in the mainstream of our economic, political and social life." In relation to this gospel demand to be critical of established institutions, and the mainstream assumption that justice can be achieved by trusting experts and tinkering with existing institutions, the brief issued a ringing call for conversion:

> We are talking about more than simple reformism and calling for more than mere individual conversion. We are calling for a conversion within our social and economic structures whereby policy making and decision making will begin to reflect and make practical the values of justice, dignity and fulfilment for every human being. Our corporate sins must be acknowledged and we must turn around, if we are to have a society that truly reflects the social consequences of the New Commandment. To bless the established order is to remain unconverted![6]

In other briefs Project North also invoked biblical precedents to defend both the churches' involvement in public policy debates and their decision to be in solidarity with native peoples. In their presentation to the President's Council on Environmental Quality in

Washington on May 24, 1977, on behalf of Project North, Russell Hatton and Hugh McCullum explained "why the churches have involved themselves in what appears to be essentially a political and economic issue." They pointed out "that questions of justice are as important, indeed more important, than economic questions and that the churches must hold up the biblical and evangelical tradition where to know God is to seek justice, human dignity and fulfilment for every human being."[7] Whereas in the past the churches had sided with the established order in its efforts to assimilate natives, they now sided with the natives in their struggle for control over their lands. As further grounds for rejecting the pipeline and supporting the natives, the story of the good Samaritan was recalled.

> We . . . suggest that to pass by on the other side means to fail to deal squarely with the issues of justice in respect to Native land claims and the cultural, political and economic survival of the Native peoples of the Northwest Territories and the Yukon; that it means irresponsible stewardship with respect to the exploitation of energy and mineral resources north of the 60th parallel; that it means to denigrate our human and natural resources; above all, that it is to deny justice, dignity and human fulfillment for all God's people.[8]

Later Project North briefs spelled out in even more detail the biblical background of the churches' involvement in justice issues as well as the biblical basis for supporting native peoples in their struggles against resource development schemes. The June 1977 brief to the Alaska Highway Pipeline Inquiry repeated earlier claims about God's sovereignty over all realms of life and identified critics of the pipeline proposal with the prophetic tradition. "As Christians, we stand in the tradition of the prophets of Israel where it was understood that people came to know God by seeking justice for the disinherited, the poor, and the oppressed." Thus, "We are called to act in solidarity with native peoples and others engaged in the struggles for justice in Canada." Since they also stood "in the tradition of the Scriptures where God is understood to be the Lord of creation" it was imperative "to see that responsible stewardship is exercised in the development of Canada's resources."[9]

Project North's 1981 brief to the National Energy Board in connection with the Norman Wells oil pipeline application provided an even more detailed account of their biblical warrants. In response to a question about the general objectives and programs of Project North, they said:

First, the basic purposes are rooted in the biblical tradition of socio-economic justice and responsible stewardship of resources. By social and economic justice we refer to a central theme in the Scriptures in which Yahweh is understood as the God who defends the poor, the downtrodden, the weak and the oppressed (e.g., Deuteronomy 15:4-11; 24:14-15; Exodus 22:22-25; Leviticus 19:13). To know God, therefore, entails seeking justice for the poor and the oppressed (e.g., Matthew 25:31-46; Mark 10:42-45; Luke 4:18-20; James 2:1-13; Amos, Jeremiah, Hosea, Micah, etc.). By responsible stewardship of resources, we refer to those themes in the Scriptures wherein men and women are charged by God with the responsibility of being the custodians and caretakers of Creation (e.g., Colossians 1:15-20; Isaiah 24:1-12; Jeremiah 34:8-17). The resources of the earth are to be developed, caringly and sparingly, to serve the Native People for a more fully human life (e.g., Leviticus 25:1-7, 23-28; Luke 4:16-22; Amos 5:11).[10]

Not surprisingly, church members who were critical of the call for a moratorium did not appreciate Project North's claim that opponents of the pipeline had the Christian tradition on their side. They were even more distressed by the assumption that unconverted defenders of the pipeline had subordinated their ethical concerns and religious values to a materialistic, environmentally destructive quest for corporate profits and wasteful patterns of consumption.[11] As one reporter rather facetiously put it: "They [the church leaders and religious groups supporting the call for a moratorium] have the stern bit of righteousness between their teeth and the onus is now on the morally suspect pro-pipeliners to prove that Christ lives in them too."[12]

Defenders of the pipeline were quite sure that Christ lived in them as well, and that it was the pro-moratorium church leaders and church activists who had strayed from a secure grounding in either the biblical faith or the beliefs of the majority of their members and financial supporters. In a letter to the Primate of the Anglican Church, the Chairman of Arctic Gas explicitly rejected the claim that critics such as himself thought that the church should not be involved in public debates. His concern was that on this issue the churches were misguided.[13] In a similar fashion, the author of the "Business Replies" article introduced in Chapter 2, and Canon Ivany, who was quoted in the previous chapter, spoke for many business people when they suggested that it was the anti-pipeline church leaders who should be called to account.

What is of particular interest in this chapter is the way the author of the "Church Speaks" article was challenged on his use of scripture. The businessman complained that the Bible had been quoted, "not only in an attempt to justify the right of the church to take political action, but also to imply the correctness of that action." One quotation that caught his attention was: "Woe to those who lay house to house and land to land, and grind the faces of the poor." Could not such a passage be used to support a variety of economic views? From a business point of view, it was church activism in the North that had contributed to unemployment and poverty, "which are grinding indeed to the poor." Was it not embarrassing that one of the church leaders most critical of the businesses which were trying to provide jobs and dignity for natives would quote scriptures telling business people that causing poverty is morally wrong?[14]

The businessman assumed that relating what the prophets had done in their context to what Christians should do in the twentieth century must surely involve more than citing passages from the Bible. "What is needed is a good deal of fresh scholarship to determine ways biblical theology can be applied with integrity and intelligence in an age of technical and moral contexts far different from anything known before." Meanwhile, he said, "it is not helpful to have verses of Scripture quoted in an attempt to foreclose a debate before it is really under way."[15]

Persons for whom the businessman was speaking were critical of the churches' preoccupation with social issues at a time when fewer and fewer people were turning to the churches for the spiritual nurture which they could surely expect the churches to provide. This did not mean, however, that they thought that religion was a purely private matter and that the world should be left in secular hands. In their view:

> Life is at its best when the secular is inspired by the sacred—that is when our politics, culture, and commerce are informed by the values of religious faith. Thus men and women in business are helped to understand that in an ultimate sense the purpose of economic activity is not pure and selfish ambition but human improvement.
> Like David, whose dance was done for the Lord, business people also have a vocation that may be offered for the glory of God.[16]

The author of the "Church Speaks" article had said: "The Church that does not stand within the prophetic tradition as part of its spiritual and faith commitment is not true to its biblical roots."[17]

Defenders of the pipeline had a twofold response to this claim. On the one hand, as the businessman observed, one could locate oneself within the prophetic tradition with its concern for the poor and still decide that the pipeline would be a good thing. The second line of argument open to them was that there are different strands of biblical faith. For example, there are two covenant traditions, one which can be traced back to the liberation struggle led by Moses, and another running forward from the covenants with Abraham and Noah to the kingly rule of David. According to Walter Brueggemann:

> the Mosaic tradition tends to be a movement of protest which is situated among the disinherited and which articulates its theological vision in terms of a God who decisively intrudes, even against seemingly impenetrable institutions and orderings. On the other hand, the Davidic tradition tends to be a movement of consolidation which is situated among the established and secure and which articulates its theological vision in terms of a God who faithfully abides and sustains on behalf of the present ordering.[18]

The obvious fit between Project North and the liberationist, prophetic tradition is not unrelated to the fact that Brueggemann devised the typology from a liberationist perspective. He was reacting against the tendency of mainstream biblical scholars to assume that their reconstructions of biblical history which ignored the significance of social class and power were politically neutral, while scholars such as Norman Gottwald who took a more sociological approach were reflecting a Marxist bias. By tracing the recurrent tension between prophetic religion and the religion of the rulers through different periods of Israel's history, he was able to show that both dissent from and affirmation of the existing order were parts of the biblical tradition. A decade later the tables have been turned. Liberation theologians and exegetes now tend to give the impression that theirs is the only correct reading of the scriptures. I am therefore using Brueggemann's discussion of the Mosaic and Davidic trajectories to suggest that even if defenders of the pipeline were also defenders of the established order they could, as the author of the "Business Replies" article said, be like David and offer their vocations for the glory of God.

Many of the defenders of the pipeline who criticized the churches' anti-development stance did, in fact, in letters, articles and interviews affirm the legitimacy of the existing social order. They talked about the need for orderly development in the North, the legitimate energy needs of the South, and the need for natives to adapt to the advancing technological society. After their initial tendency to say that the churches should stay out of politics, most critics of the churches' anti-pipeline stance agreed that the churches had a right to be involved. The problem was that on this issue the churches were wrong. They were wrong because they had their facts wrong. Ignorance of the facts, in turn, led to faulty understandings of the consequences of what they were proposing. The policies they were promoting would cause rather than relieve poverty. The anti-pipeline and anti-development church leaders and activists were also wrong at the ideological level. As the author of the "Business Replies" article said, they were attacking "the economic philosophy that we [business people] sincerely believe to be in the best interests of Canada."[19]

The other group of church people who disagreed with the call for a moratorium, and who were critical of Project North's style of operation, did not seem anxious to defend the established order. They insisted that they were not pro-development, and they agreed that Canada needed an alternative energy policy. There should be a just settlement of native claims, but that belief was shared, not only with Project North, but with most of the pro-pipeline church members. This group stressed that, since there were church people on both sides of the issue, the churches should play a reconciling rather than a divisive role. They also felt that, in contrast to Project North's exclusive commitment to particular groups, the churches should be concerned about the spiritual and material welfare of all Northerners. Typical representatives of this position were the members of the United Church's Northern Co-ordinating Committee; John Sperry, Anglican Bishop of the Arctic; and the lay Catholic business people in Calgary, who carried on a vigorous series of exchanges with the Social Action Department of the Canadian Conference of Catholic Bishops. Similar views were expressed by Lutherans who felt that the churches should focus on their primary responsibilities for spiritual nurture, and the Mennonite Brethren who worried that the Mennonite Central Committee, which supported Project North, was placing too much emphasis on Jesus as Lord, and not enough on Jesus as Saviour.

When the Project North team and its pro-development and pastorally oriented critics created occasions to discuss their differences, attention did not appear to be focused on what the Bible said or how it should be interpreted. What such meetings clearly revealed was that different definitions of the problem and conflicting attitudes towards the pipeline were deeply rooted in different experiences, different responsibilities and different loyalties. Rather than helping to transcend these differences, appeals to the Bible seemed to deepen the divisions and make lay members feel even more alienated from church leaders. This was unfortunate, because I do not think that church leaders intended to use the Bible that way. I believe that a closer look at how appeals to the Bible and to religious convictions were actually used will show how they did contribute, and could have contributed more effectively, to the framework within which the debate proceeded.

2. Foundation vs. Scaffolding[20]

I introduced the idea that Project North and its pro-pipeline critics reflected affinities with different trajectories of biblical faith to highlight the fact that appeals to the Bible or to the Christian tradition did not provide a simple way to resolve disagreements over the pipeline. I will return once again to the "Church Speaks—Business Replies" exchange to clarify what seems to have been going on when the Bible was appealed to as a source of authority. We saw that the author of the "Business Replies" article thought that the church leader was quoting scripture to foreclose a debate that was not yet really under way. What did the church leader himself think he was doing?

On the one hand, he did link the claim that Jesus was on the side of the poor and oppressed, and the fact that natives were poor and oppressed, to the conclusion both that the church had a right to ask questions about northern development and that the Christian thing to do would be to oppose the pipeline. On the other hand, he no doubt did not intend to be unfair to the business people who were faithful Christians. He was making it clear that his own ethical choices were grounded in a desire to be a faithful follower of Jesus, and he expected others, including those church members who disagreed with him, to do the same. "Sometimes we may be out of step with one another, but I hope at least our loyalty lies in the same direction—and for the rest we can work it out together."[21]

As far as the pipeline debate was concerned, working it out together could involve discussing concrete issues, such as whether or not the pipeline was needed and what impact a pipeline would have on native communities, at factual and ethical levels of clarification. It could also involve attempting to have a more disciplined debate about the merits of that economic philosophy which business people think is in the best interests of Canada, or about the wisdom of trying to create an alternative society based on conserver rather than consumer values.[22] Thus, stating his religious beliefs along with the other factors he took into account was a way to clarify where he was coming from and why he was taking the stand he was. It was not intended to stop the debate with an appeal to an overriding religious authority.

There might seem to be a paradox here. If religious beliefs have to do with our deepest convictions about reality and about what it means to be human should they not have overriding authority for our decisions? The apparent paradox can be resolved by noticing that religious absolutes operate at a very general level. The claim that everyone is of equal worth, and that God is on the side of those whose worth has been denied through unjust social structures, leaves open a number of questions regarding what ought to be done in a particular case to affirm someone's worth. Should a pipeline be built that will create jobs, or should it be blocked because it would damage communities? Most participants in the debate agreed with basic absolutes regarding justice for native peoples and responsible development of non-renewable resources. However, they had different understandings of what followed from these basic beliefs regarding particular policies. If the church leader had concluded that his loyalties and those of his critics did not in fact lie in the same direction, he would have found himself in a different situation. He would have had to reassess what he was up against, and, if debate could take place at all, it would be necessary to clarify underlying convictions. Even in a situation such as that, however, it seems likely that the most useful appeals to scripture and tradition would be those designed to draw out the other party and to keep the debate going. The least useful would be the type of appeal to scriptural authority which gave the other party the impression that the debate had been foreclosed before it had really gotten under way.

Project North's brief to the Berger Inquiry has already been viewed from different angles. I will now look more closely at how appeals to the Bible and to religious convictions were used in that brief. My particular interest is in the difference between assuming that appeals to scripture and tradition can be used to resolve disputes and treating them as contributions to the scaffolding required for the debate to proceed.

The brief insisted that decisions about the pipeline "must be considered along moral and ethical grounds at least as equally as political and economic grounds, because we are talking about the soul of the nation."[23] Unless moral and ethical issues were dealt with explicitly, the pipeline would appear to represent development, and development would be defined in relation to priorities so embedded in existing institutions that they are simply taken for granted. The problem with the existing social order is that more priority is given "to economic growth and profit-oriented values (which are called 'realities') and less to social justice and human dignity (which are called 'humanitarian sentiments')." That understanding of reality is based on the assumption that economic growth produces higher levels of justice and human well-being. The brief was challenging that assumption. "In our experience we are discovering that justice and human dignity are not the automatic by-products of such economic growth."[24]

On the one hand, the brief implied that justice and human dignity were shared goals, and that disagreement was over the extent to which a growth-oriented market economy was achieving these goals. On the other hand, there was a tendency to imply that those who wanted to build a pipeline against the wishes of natives were not committed to justice and human dignity. Because there was a clear link in their own case between calling for a moratorium, being "in solidarity with the Native Peoples of Canada," and extending "the love of God in Christ" to "all realms of life," it was easy to give the impression that denying one link in this chain was to deny them all.[25] They would not, however, have directly defended the claim that church members who wanted to build the pipeline were not trying to extend the love of God in Christ to all realms of life. Insofar as they were challenging pro-pipeline Christians to show how building the pipeline was consistent with their claims to respect the rights of natives, and with their desire to extend God's love into all realms of life, the authors of the brief were using appeals to scripture and tradition to broaden the framework within which the debate was proceeding.

In their appeals to the Bible, the authors of the Project North brief were relying, not on its authority to end the debate, but on the disclosive power of biblical symbols and stories to help Canadians to imagine a new future. They were appealing to scripture to open up the debate so that basic issues would be confronted. The following passage illustrates both their "post-liberal" understanding of religious doctrine,[26] and their emphasis on the future-oriented, transforming power of the gospel:

> The Gospel is more than mere propositions. The Good News is a cluster of living images and values for living. It brings with it a radically new vision of man. In view of this new vision of man, Christians are called to take a critical stance regarding the social reality of each time and space. The Gospel sheds critical light on corporations and calls into question many of the images and norms which prevail in the mainstream of our economic, political and social life.[27]

The critical light shed by the gospel on the prevailing norms and practices of governments and corporations did not in itself produce certainty regarding particular policies. For example, when the Métis and the Dene took different approaches to the pipeline and land claim issues, the churches were forced to acknowledge that criteria other than solidarity with native peoples were required to clarify and defend their actions. During the summer of 1976, the Métis and the Dene were unable to produce a shared land claim proposal. The federal government withdrew funding in the hopes of forcing the groups back together. Both organizations appealed to the churches for emergency support. Without wishing to take sides in an internal dispute, the Anglican and Roman Catholic churches decided to provide emergency loans and grants to the Dene.

Church leaders defended their decision to provide emergency financial support for the 1976 Dene Assembly on the grounds that it was a crucial part of the Dene struggle for a general land claim settlement. The Dene wanted to meet the federal government's November 1 deadline without abandoning their demand that no major resource projects be approved until a settlement had been reached. The Métis, however, had abandoned any hope that native claims would be settled before the pipeline was built. They therefore wanted to negotiate benefits from the pipeline rather than continuing their attempt to block it.

According to the prophetic wing of the churches, the Dene were pointing the way to a new and more environmentally responsible future. They were fighting not only their own but the South's battle against a mindless commitment to economic growth for growth's sake. As Clifton Monk, Lutheran representative on the Project North Administrative Committee, told a Lutheran Conference on Ministry in the North, confronting established powers with a vision of a new future was a central part of the prophetic task. He cited Walter Brueggemann's claim that: "It is the vocation of the prophet to keep on conjuring and proposing alternative futures to the single one the King wants to urge as the only thinkable one."[28]

Project North's appeal to the Bible and to religious convictions to support their stance must be seen in relation to all of the other factors taken into account and all of the judgments made at the various levels of clarification. The differences between Project North and its establishment-oriented and pastorally concerned critics were deeply embedded in the details of their differing definitions of the problem, their different perceptions about conditions in the North and the needs of northerners, and so forth.[29] Although there is a place for arguing about what can or cannot legitimately be claimed to be in continuity with biblical faith, such arguments often simply divert attention away from the real issues which divide and unite different groups. The experiences the McCullums and other members of the Project North team had at Dene Assemblies, and in other deeply moving sessions during which the young Dene leaders, the elders and the rest of the Dene struggled to formulate their demands, profoundly influenced how they saw the pipeline debate. Similarly, other church people, such as the Presbyterian leaders whose stories were introduced in Chapter Two, the Anglican Bishop of the Arctic, and the members of the United Church's Northern Co-ordinating Committee, reflected the influence of a different set of experiences and relationships.

One United Church staff person interviewed for this study was critical of Project North's confrontational style, since it undermined the trust that had been built up between church leaders and the boardrooms of the corporations. From the standpoint of Project North's prophetic stance this desire in itself reflected a high level of accommodation to the established order. The United Church staff person, on the other hand, was genuinely concerned about living conditions for the workers. He believed that something important had been accomplished when the companies had agreed to change their work schedules in a way that benefited the workers. He was concerned that it would be more difficult to make these gains if persons working for governments and corporations were treated as the enemy by other church-sponsored groups. These differences in outlook were certainly related to different understandings of the biblical roots of their faith. It is quite obvious that the differences between Project North and this staff person could not be resolved by attempts to win each other over to the correct reading of the Bible. However, turning to their biblical roots as part of their stories rather than as an authority the other should find binding could have had a unifying rather than divisive impact on their discussions. Unfortunately the temptation to use the Bible to foreshorten rather than to facilitate discussion is hard to resist.

My growing awareness that the movement through different levels of clarification leads back to the stories of the participants rather than towards foundational bedrock has affected my understanding of the method I have been using in this study. I used to assume that the movement through the different levels of clarification involved going from initial stories to analyses of claims and counter-claims regarding facts, consequences, rights and ideologies and on to the clarification of foundations as the final step on the way to decision and action. I now find it more useful to follow the movements that participants in a debate actually seem to make from initial stories to analysis and back to the stories which shape who we are and how we act. At the post-ethical level of clarification identities are clarified and foundational concerns are identified and discussed. These foundational convictions add depth and scope to the framework within which disciplined debate proceeds. They do not, in spite of the impression often given, provide the bedrock on the basis of which debate-stopping pronouncements are made.[30] I will return to this claim in my concluding reflections on the framework which allows prophets and pastors to debate public choices, and which facilitates the move from reflection on to further action.

Notes

1. Project North, "A Call for a Moratorium," in *Canadian Churches and Social Justice*, ed. John Williams (Toronto: Anglican Book Centre and James Lorimer, 1984), pp. 155-67.

2. Canadian church leaders, "Justice Demands Action: A Statement of Concern to the Prime Minister and Cabinet," in *Do Justice! The Social Teaching of the Canadian Catholic Bishops*, ed. E.F. Sheridan, S.J. (Sherbrooke and Toronto: Éditions Paulines and The Jesuit Centre for Social Faith and Justice, 1987), pp. 300-302.

3. Project North, "A Call for a Moratorium," in Williams, *Canadian Churches*, p. 156.

4. Ibid., p. 156.

5. Ibid., p. 157.

6. Ibid., pp. 157-58.

7. Project North: A Canadian Interchurch Project on Northern Development, "A Summary Statement to the President's Council on Environmental Quality," Executive Office of the President, Washington, D.C., 24 May 1977, p. 3.

8. Ibid., p. 4.

9. "Statement of Evidence by Project North before the Alaska Highway Pipeline Inquiry in Whitehorse, Yukon, June 1977," p. 2.

10. Project North, "Before the National Energy Board in the Matter of the Norman Wells Oil Pipeline Application (1981)," in Williams, *Canadian Churches*, p. 169.

11. See Hugh and Karmel McCullum, *This Land Is Not For Sale* (Toronto: Anglican Book Centre, 1975), p. 26.

12. Jon Ferry, "Pipeline Foes United: Different Philosophies but Common Cause," The *Edmonton Journal*, 7 May 1977.

13. William Wilder to Archbishop Edward Scott, 5 October 1976. General Synod Archives.

14. "Business Replies: 'Using the Church to Promote a One-sided Economic View,' " *The United Church Observer*, August 1978, p. 21.

15. Ibid., p. 21.

16. Ibid., p. 19.

17. "Church Speaks: 'Firmly on the Side of the Poor,' " *The United Church Observer*, August 1978, p. 17.

18. Walter Brueggemann, "Trajectories in Old Testament Literature and the Sociology of Ancient Israel," *Journal of Biblical Literature*, 98 (1979): 162.

19. "Business Replies," p. 20.

20. Linell Cady, "Foundation vs. Scaffolding: The Possibility of Justification in an Historical Approach to Ethics," *Union Seminary Quarterly Review*, 41, 2 (1987): 45-62.

21. "Church Speaks," p. 18.

22. For an interesting analysis of the pipeline debate from the standpoint of the root metaphors underlying different stances, see Gibson Winter, *Liberating Creation: Foundations of Religious Social Ethics* (New York: Crossroad, 1981). During the early stages of this study, Winter and I co-authored papers on the pipeline debate for the 1979 meetings of the American Association for the Advancement of Science and a 1981 World Council of Churches Consultation on Political Ethics.

23. Project North, "A Call for a Moratorium," in Williams, *Canadian Churches*, p. 156.

24. Ibid., p. 157.

25. Ibid., pp. 156-58.

26. George Lindbeck, *The Nature of Doctrine: Religion and Theology in a Post-Liberal Age* (Philadelphia: Westminster Press, 1984).

27. Project North, "A Call for a Moratorium," in Williams, *Canadian Churches*, p. 157. See also James Gustafson's comments about theology as a way of construing the world in *Ethics from a Theocentric Perspective: Volume One, Theology and Ethics* (Chicago: The University of Chicago Press, 1981), p. 158.

28. Clifton L. Monk, "Social and Economic Justice as Ministry in the North," paper presented at the Inter-Lutheran Ministry Conference, Edmonton, Alberta, 4-5 May 1982, p. 4. The quotation from Brueggemann is from *The Prophetic Imagination* (Philadelphia: Fortress Press, 1978), p. 45.

29. See Jeffrey Stout's contribution to the symposium on *Habits of the Heart*, "Liberal Society and the Language of Morals," in *Soundings*, 49, 1-2 (Spring/Summer 1986): 37: "Brian's justification of his life does not, as the authors think, rest on a 'fragile foundation' (8), for it does not rest on a foundation at all. It rests in the details of his story. It is by telling his story and implicitly invoking its evaluative framework that Brian initially understands his life and justifies his current commitments as superior to his old ones."

30. Francis Schüssler Fiorenza, *Foundational Theology: Jesus and the Church* (New York: Crossroad, 1986), p. 46: "This foundational task is not, as the term might suggest, that of the builder laying a foundation in bedrock or that of the archaeologist digging down to the lowest stratum but that of the interpreter seeking to convey the meaning of a past event and experience, seeking to translate its illuminative and liberating vision, and seeking to elucidate its transformative consequences for human life."

Conclusion

The Mackenzie Valley pipeline debate was not just about a pipeline. It was about the future of the North and of the people who live there. As Project North said in its brief, the debate raised questions about the soul of the nation. It was, however, also about whether or not a pipeline was needed, and about how to count trappers and to assess the value of country food. The ethical and religious dimensions of the debate were as integrally related to the latter questions, in spite of their secular appearance, as to the former, in spite of their more commonly recognized connection with morality and religion. The claims and counter-claims encountered at each level of clarification have their own points of contact with reality.

There is a sense in which the role of reflection is to help us to move from the surface encounters of our initial definitions of the problem through different levels of analysis to a deeper grasp of the stories which shape who we are and how we act. However, there is another sense in which the surface to depth imagery is misleading. It gives the impression that we move from stories through empirical and rational analysis to foundations which are most directly related to reality. We are probably as in touch with reality when we are telling our stories as when we are attempting to articulate our most basic convictions. The glimpses of reality which guide our actions are sometimes embedded in stories; sometimes expressed as the hard facts of scientific demonstration; and sometimes presented as consequences or rights claims, or as arguments based upon our vision of a better world.

What we decide to do in the present, and how we think we ought to have acted in the past, involve a holistic appraisal of the whole range of relevant factors. The challenge we all face, therefore, is how to relate story-telling, rigorous analysis and confessions of our deepest convictions to the judgments we make about complex issues of public policy. The main feature of the method I have been using in this study has been the identification of different levels of analysis. Sorting out the debate in this way has served two purposes. First, it has helped to align the claims made by one side in a debate with the counter-claims made by the other side. Communication is often distorted and unsuccessful in our public debates because participants are like ships passing in the night. To use an image from my engineering background, the claims and counter-claims of different participants are often not "geared in" with one another. They do not mesh and yield fruitful exchanges. The aim of identifying different levels of clarification is to see that stories were matched against stories; claims about the facts were "geared in" to challenges to those claims; and arguments about consequences, rights and ideologies were brought into line with one another.

In addition to this horizontal use of the levels, there was also a vertical use. Identifying different levels of discourse helped to illumine the internal coherence and the profile of each position. Not surprisingly, the kinds of facts that were cited, and the kinds of ethical arguments that were used (consequentialist, rights language, ideology critique) were already embedded in the stories through which initial definitions of the problem were reported.

It was this internal consistency within each position which made it possible to characterize different groups as "prophetic," "establishment-oriented" and "pastorally concerned." The identities of these groups were shaped by different experiences and loyalties, different ways of defining the problem and different ways of addressing the issue of the pipeline. Different types of discourse were aimed at different audiences and designed to perform different functions. At some moments in their presentations to the Berger Inquiry or the National Energy Board participants were attempting to persuade commissioners, politicians and the general public of the rightness of their causes by alluding to connections between the community's values and a proponent's or a "public interest" group's conclusions about the pipeline. At other times they were trying to convince lawyers and other experts of particular points through rigorous demonstration of facts and logically sound arguments. Thus far in the study I have used the identification of different levels of clarification to provide an orderly reconstruction of the debate. As a final step I will look back at the debate, and at my analysis of the debate, not only to review the roles of the different levels of clarification, but also from the standpoint of different modes of discourse which are related to but not identical with the levels of clarification.

1. Varieties of Moral Discourse

In a recent analysis of the social ethical writings of the Church and Society Sub-Unit of the World Council of Churches, James Gustafson reported that he had found examples of prophetic, narrative, ethical and policy discourse.[1] He observed that each type of discourse had a certain legitimacy, but that ecumenical work on social ethics would be enhanced by a higher level of self-consciousness about which type was being used to address what audience at a particular point in time. The same thing could be said for the pipeline debate. On the one hand, as a prophetic movement mandated to be in solidarity with native groups struggling for justice, Project North was an exciting venture in ecumenical co-operation. The prophetic witness of Project North launched a new era in the relations between the mainstream Christian churches and native peoples. Its prophetic discourse struck a clear and decisive note at a moment in Canadian history when the northern natives were pitted in a David and Goliath struggle against the combined power of the federal government and the world's largest oil companies. On the other hand, the prophet's critiques of established power and demands for conversion are sometimes unnecessarily strident and uncompromising.

Prophetic denunciations of established institutions and absolute demands for a new future tend to heighten differences between prophetic minorities and the middle-class church members whose support, financial and otherwise, enables mainstream churches to sponsor such activities. By focusing on "the root of the evil [prophetic witness] cannot inform incremental choices made by persons and institutions where good and bad are commingled, and where 'trade-offs' have to be defended." By focusing on "an ideal future," prophetic discourse "often has little to say about means to shorter range ends in view."[2] Thus, Project North knew that it must speak other languages as well. Its brief to the Berger Inquiry defended "the feasibility of such a moratorium not only at the moral and ethical level but at what the government and oil companies like to describe as the 'practical' or 'realistic' or 'pragmatic' level."[3] In addition to prophetic and pragmatic ways of speaking, Project North used a narrative mode of discourse as well.

Different degrees of appreciation for the role of story-telling was most dramatically demonstrated by different reactions to Berger's decision to hold community hearings without formal presentations of evidence or cross-examination of witnesses. The native organizations requested this format and the churches enthusiastically endorsed the idea. Arctic Gas lawyers, and social scientists such as Stabler and Olfert, were less convinced that such stories and nostalgic remembrances would produce usable and relevant data or insights. As Gustafson points out, narratives perform different functions. They "sustain common memory in a community" and "shape the moral ethos of a community and provide its moral identity." It was that function that Stabler and Olfert belittled. A further use is that, "Telling an apt story may provide more nuanced and subtle illumination at that moment than the conclusion of a rigorous casuistic argument."[4]

The persuasive power of narrative was illustrated over and over again as natives spoke in their own languages and in their own way about what the pipeline meant to them. Berger incorporated opportunities for the use of narrative discourse into the Inquiry because personal stories, carefully documented empirical findings of various kinds of experts, and rigorously defended arguments would all be taken into account. Insights gained from stories would be considered when it was finally time to exercise human judgment and to decide how the evidence and arguments added up for and against the pipeline. Such stories were neither reduced to irrelevance nor given overriding authority to determine action. They had a legitimate contribution to make to the process of practical reasoning in which the Inquiry was engaged.[5]

I noted in the previous chapter that Project North's use of the Bible should be seen as an attempt to broaden the framework within which the debate was taking place rather than as a debate-stopping appeal to authoritatively grounded truth claims. That is, the use of the Bible evoked a common memory that God cares for the oppressed and for the resources of the earth. Project North was tapping the disclosive power of biblical stories and symbols to generate an openness to new possibilities and to call into question existing assumptions and priorities. These appeals created a moral ethos in which only barbarians would refuse to care about justice for natives and stewardship of non-renewable resources. What offended some of the industry personnel, therefore, was the implied charge that they did not care about native people or the environment.

Although the narrative portion of the brief dealing with the biblical precedents for the churches' stance was intended to elicit agreement that native rights and environmental concerns must be taken seriously, the claims in this section were not to be taken literally.[6] It is for this reason that such sections of church briefs often appear to be empty rhetoric to other participants in a debate, including many church members. It also explains why church leaders seemed surprised when business people thought that they personally were being accused of racism, colonialism and unChristian conduct. The business people did not know that the church leaders' words were not meant to be taken literally!

Paying explicit attention to narrative discourse, and to the initial story-telling step in the method I am using in this study, brings to light an interesting phenomenon. On the one hand, church representatives vigorously defended the natives' right to tell their stories, and took it for granted that Berger must hear the churches' story in order to understand why they were intervening in a political debate. On the other hand, spokespersons for Project North seemed quite willing to make judgments about, and to impute motives to, their establishment-oriented or pastorally concerned critics without hearing their stories. Some members of the United Church's Northern Co-ordinating Committee who were in daily contact with natives were offended when they were told by Project North staff that they should talk to natives. The implication was that they were being told to talk to the right natives, but there was also a suggestion that their criticisms of Project North must result from a lack of contact of any kind with natives. In order to have an opportunity to hear one another's stories, it is necessary to have settings such as the community hearings in which all participants can be assured that their stories will be heard.

Narrative discourse has an important place in public debates, and there can be direct links between a revealing story and appropriate action. However, there are times when stories must be questioned and when narratives must be analysed. As Gustafson points out, it is proper "in the intellectual moral life of the church to make ethical, indeed casuistic, arguments for the propriety of one story in relation to another."[7] The main task of this study has been to show how different participants in the debate moved beyond telling their stories to defend their proposals in relation to different perceptions of the facts, different understandings of what northern natives desire and deserve, different assessments of the consequences of building or failing to build the pipeline, and different assumptions about the kind of society Canada is and should become.

The first two chapters show how a wide range of factors converged to produce a debate over the proposed Mackenzie Valley pipeline, and how responses to the proposal reflected the different worlds in which defenders and critics lived, even though in many cases they were members of the same churches. Chapters 3, 4 and 5 reconstruct different strands of the debate from the standpoint of different ways of moving from story-telling to analysis, or from narrative reports and prophetic calls for action to the documentation of claims and counter-claims and the assessments of arguments.

In Chapter 3 it was necessary to get beyond the initial impression that the debate was between realists with hard facts and idealists inspired by subjective values or, as Project North said in its brief to the Berger Inquiry, "humanistic sentiments." In the first place, the churches and other public interest groups took seriously the need to back up their claim that the pipeline was not needed with carefully documented facts and well-constructed arguments. Second, they demonstrated the relevance of questions which normally lie beyond the terms of reference of the National Energy Board. Why, for example, should it simply be assumed that the energy intensive way of life of southern Canadians should be protected while the native communities are expected to adapt to the disruptions caused by a pipeline?

Chapters 4 and 5 taken together show how my initial guess that Berger took for granted a consequentialist or utilitarian framework for the debate needed to be modified. The recent history of moral reasoning by Jonsen and Toulmin, which was published after I had completed the first six chapters of this study, has helped me to see more clearly than I did before the connection between Berger's approach and casuistical thinking. Until I read Jonsen and Toulmin's *The Abuse of Casuistry*, I had unwittingly shared the modern assumption that casuistry was clever but false reasoning. I see now, however, obvious continuities between what I have been describing as comparative ethics and that earlier tradition which starts with cases, takes circumstances and diversity of opinion into account, and acknowledges the role of human judgment in moving from diverse opinions to decision and action.

Jonsen and Toulmin rediscovered the importance of a case approach to practical moral reasoning when they worked together on the US Congress' National Commission for the Protection of Human Subjects of Biomedical and Behavioral Research. Members of that Commission were able to achieve an amazing degree of agreement as long as they focused on concrete problems. When attention shifted from *what* was being proposed to *why* different members agreed or disagreed, differences in background and theoretical orientation became relevant and divisive. If they had attempted to reach consensus at the level of background theories, religious convictions and ideological orientations the work of the Commission would have ground to a halt.

It was a further insight, however, that prompted Jonsen and Toulmin to write a book on casuistry. The case method which was a central feature of the Commission's success, and the resulting "casuistry (or moral taxonomy) for distinguishing acceptable from unacceptable ways of involving humans as subjects in medical or behavioral research," reflected an approach to practical moral reasoning that was quite foreign to "current ethical theory."[8] As the result of developments in Western patterns of thought which Jonsen and Toulmin trace back to Pascal and Descartes, philosophers, with notable exceptions, have turned their attention to "abstract theoretical issues in isolation from concrete problems, practical issues, and actual circumstances." Casuistry declined within the Catholic Church as well. By the end of the nineteenth century, issues such as contraception were being dealt with by the Holy Office "not by debate but by decree."[9]

A case approach to practical moral reasoning, which takes into account actual circumstances and diversity of opinion but which also moves towards decision and action, has been kept alive by novelists, dramatists, physicians, lawyers, judges, pastors and others who attend concretely to actual human experience. It is enjoying a revival in medical ethics and in church statements which result from open processes of discussion and debate. However, there is a serious lack, according to Jonsen and Toulmin, of the necessary institutional settings for this type of moral reasoning. In Canada, such settings have been provided by public inquiries such as the Berger Commission and the hearings of the National Energy Board. This tradition of practical moral reasoning has also been practised by participants in these inquiries, such as the churches which have fostered open discussion and debate in the formulation of their own positions.

There are obvious affinities between the consequentialist framework within which Asch, Hobart and Berger carried on their extended exchanges and the casuistical case approach described by Jonsen and Toulmin. Asch, Hobart and Berger defined the problem precisely, and developed finely tuned distinctions between trappers and non-trappers, exchange values and replacement values, and so forth. The practical problem they kept clearly in focus was whether or not the pipeline should be built. As specific contributions to this large decision, answerable questions were framed which could be pursued with empirical rigor. In order to make a recommendation about the pipeline it was necessary to determine what existed and how present conditions would be affected by a pipeline. In keeping with his training as a trial lawyer and his experience as a judge, Berger knew that his final recommendation would neither be inferred from a single overridingly important factual claim nor deduced from a universal moral principle. It would follow, rather, "from the accumulation of many and varied supporting reasons." The "casuistical argument" he eventually presented resembled "the rhetorical and commonsense discourse that piles up many kinds of argument in hopes of showing the favoured position in a good light." As Jonsen and Toulmin point out, "the 'weight' of a casuistical opinion came from the accumulation of reasons rather than from the logical validity of the arguments or the coherence of any single 'proof.' "[10]

Hobart was comfortable with the role of the detached scientist who presented the facts for someone else to weigh in the balance with all of the other factors that would finally enter into the decision. He assumed that the pipeline would be a good thing because, as he put it, the bottom line for him was that the land could no longer support the native population. Asch was less hesitant to claim that social scientists have stances whether they are aware of them or not. That should not, however, pre-determine their findings. He supported the Dene demand for a moratorium and for self-determination because that was the most reasonable solution to the enormous problems of the Mackenzie Valley. He did not invoke the right to self-determination as an abstract, universal principle as the basis for his judgment. For him self-determination was a contextual value, not a transcendental value like peace or justice.[11] The case for Dene self-determination rested on the accumulation of evidence that there was a traditional economy that deserved to be strengthened, that employment from the pipeline would be short-term and have questionable benefits, and that conventional economic methods used to determine who would have to go on welfare and who would receive a subsidy or a tax break or a business incentive were biased against native hunters and trappers. He questioned Hobart's acculturation model because it affected how Hobart projected his findings into the future. It made the assimilation of natives and the disappearance of a traditional economy appear to be irreversible and complete. He did not, however, believe that attention should be diverted from the practical issue of assessing the impact of the pipeline on native communities to a theoretical debate between academics. Berger shared this view, and urged Asch and Hobart to avoid nit-picking arguments since he already had enough lawyers picking nits!

I used the Asch-Hobart exchanges to illustrate the way in which openness to diverse opinions and conflicting expert findings can be combined with rigorous procedures designed to move towards closure. Berger was not interested in dialogue between Asch and Hobart for the sake of dialogue. As he kept telling them he wanted to find out what was going on in the North so that an informed judgment could be made about the pipeline. Closure was achieved by dealing concretely with the question of economic conditions in native communities, and by framing answerable questions such as the amount of value contributed by country food. Openness to diversity of opinion returned when attention shifted from these precisely defined questions to the larger issue of whether or not to build the pipeline. That shift involved a transition from ethical or casuistical discourse to policy discourse. However, before I move on to a consideration of policy discourse, I must ask how the churches' emphases on the rights of natives to block the pipeline, and their critiques of the pattern of development and way of life presupposed by defenders of the pipeline, related to rigorous ethical discourse.

What do we make of the fact that the churches were prepared to take a stand against the pipeline before the studies on which Berger based his conclusions were completed? Were they implying that ethical judgments could be derived directly from universal moral principles or firmly held religious convictions? The rhetoric they used often made it appear that their conclusion about the pipeline was absolutely certain and not debatable. As we saw, however, what was not negotiable was that natives were full human beings with the same rights and duties as other human beings. Since this basic right had been denied in practice in the past, and would be denied again if the natives were not allowed to participate in the decisions affecting their lives, general acceptance of this right could not simply be taken for granted. The tendency for rights claims to be presented in a strident fashion obscured the continuity between rights language and case-oriented casuistical thinking. As Jonsen and Toulmin point out, for the casuist:

> Sound judgment in resolving problems of moral practice depended on recognizing crucial resemblances and differences between new and problematic cases and available paradigmatic cases. Ethics was not a moral "geometry" in which one could "prove" that any new case fell unambiguously under some strict universal and invariable definition of, for example, courage or temperance, treachery or murder. Nor were the merits of a case formally entailed by any such definition. Rather, arriving at sound resolutions required one to see how far and in what respects the parallels between problematic cases could justify *counting them as* cases of "courage" or "treachery."[12]

The paradigmatic case for native rights supporters was the right of all "peoples" to be self-determining; natives, by analogy, should be included under the category "people"; native "peoples" in the North had not had their rights to the land extinguished through treaties or settlements; therefore, building the pipeline before native claims were settled would count as a violation of their rights. Although this might look like a purely deductive argument, it includes judgments about actual circumstances that could be and were debated. The main leap in the argument is from the claim that native rights have not been extinguished to the conclusion that the pipeline should be blocked until the claims were settled. Industry personnel saw no need to take that step, since the rights of other landowners they dealt with were limited by the government's powers of expropriation. The fact that such questions were dealt with during cross-examination supports my earlier claim that rights language was used to broaden the framework within which the debate proceeded rather than to foreshorten it.

Attempts to push the debate in a more explicitly ideological direction were also part of the churches' attempt to challenge taken-for-granted assumptions and to broaden the framework of the debate. The parallel with Brazil gave additional rhetorical force to the argument that northern natives were a threatened species whose rights and survival were at stake. Although it is hard to know how much this analogy added to the accumulation of evidence that finally convinced Berger that he could justify recommending a moratorium, it was an imaginative, attention-getting move.[13] Not everyone was convinced by the parallel. One Anglican layman reported in a letter to the Primate that he was "a little appalled to read in this morning's *Globe and Mail* the story about a group known as Project North which has, apparently with the approval of our Church, been pontificating in front of Mr. Justice Berger." He was appalled by the claim that "the way our multinationals have treated people in Brazil has something to do with the way people will be treated in the Northwest Territories."[14]

I suggested in Chapter 6 that appeals to biblical teachings and religious convictions contributed to the framework within which the debate proceeded, but that in themselves they did not provide a certain basis for resolving disputes or for choosing between stories. This does not mean that theology is not important. It simply means that theology, like ethics, is a practical rather than a theoretical discipline. As James Gustafson has said, and as the Project North brief implied, it is a way of construing the world. It is "an effort to make sense out of a very broad range of human experiences, to find some meaning in them and for them that enables persons to live and to act in coherent ways. It reaches to the limit-questions of not only human experience, but also our knowledge of nature."[15]

At a very general level all theologies which claim to be Christian challenge ways of construing the world which do not place a high value on all people and on God's created order. At more concrete levels of experience, members of the churches which sponsored Project North construed the world in ways which have been shaped by different traditions. This has not prevented them from jointly sponsoring a wide variety of social action coalitions and ecumenical agencies. Nor does this ability to work together without prior agreement about doctrines, liturgical practices and so forth represent a simple return to the slogan from the twenties that doctrine divides but service unites. It reflects a renewed conviction that working for justice is an integral part of the churches' mission, and that there are times when agreement is essential for common action and times when pluralism should be affirmed.

Within the general commitment to work for justice there are further differences in the way persons construe the world. These differences were dramatically displayed in reactions to Project North's prophetic witness by its establishment-oriented and pastorally concerned critics. It was appropriate that their main exchanges took place at the level of policy discourse rather than assuming that consensus could be, or needed to be, achieved at theoretical or ideological levels.[16]

2. Prophets, Pastors and Public Choices

A brief discussion of the shift in attention from ethical to policy discourse provides another opportunity to clarify my own stance in relation to the pipeline debate and Project North's activities. Whereas ethical discourse focuses on justifying judgments about what ought to be done, policy discourse deals more directly with policy proposals and decisions about what to do. The traditions of casuistry and liberation theology presuppose that policy discourse involves taking sides. However, my recurrent emphasis on the diversity of the Christian tradition, and on the importance of knowing when to strive for agreement and when to welcome diversity, may create the impression that I am never prepared to takes sides. My approach to comparative ethics might appear to be closer to the Sophists, who gave the impression that one side was as good as the other, than to casuists or liberationists. Jonsen and Toulmin suggest that:

> The Sophists' program relied largely on teaching techniques for setting out opposing arguments on public issues, with a seeming implication that either side could be held with equal confidence. The leading Sophist Gorgias' last book, *Double Arguments*, showed how this technique can reinforce the belief that nothing truly general can be said in ethics, so that there is nothing left to be considered apart from particular cases and situations.[17]

In contrast to this belief that either side in a debate can be held with equal confidence, I would insist that the method I have defended in this study does not rule out taking sides in a debate. My interest is not in levelling all positions, but in clarifying how persons with different orientations make judgments which involve initial hunches, empirically testable factual claims, rationally defendable value judgments, basic religious and ideological convictions, and so forth. A major emphasis of my study has been that at the level of policy discourse ethicists, like scientists and other experts, must be self-conscious and humble about the authority claimed for their policy conclusion by virtue of their special training in ethics.

My own sympathies with Project North have been clear throughout the long years I have been working on this study. In my view, the churches were right to insist that no pipeline should be built before land claims were settled, and to question the immediate construction of a pipeline which could be delayed perhaps indefinitely if exports were reduced and energy conservation measures were adopted. This preference for Project North's anti-pipeline stance is not simply a subjective leap of faith. It is a policy conclusion based upon a whole range of factors which need to be clarified and debated.

Just as the decision to build the pipeline contained an

ideological component, opposition to its construction is influenced by beliefs about the facts and ideological commitments. The aim of the method used in this study is to move public debates beyond the level of dogmatically asserted scientific findings and uncritically affirmed ideological stances to reflectively defended moral and political choices. In the case of the pipeline debate, a necessary preliminary step was the public awakening to the fact that a northern pipeline need not be viewed as the inevitable next step in the development of frontier resources.

While Arctic Gas was preparing its application to build a natural gas pipeline up the Mackenzie Valley there seemed to be little reason to doubt that this project would be welcomed as the logical extension of existing pipelines. As the massive amount of documentation submitted with the application in March of 1974 suggests, the applicants were prepared to defend the feasibility of their proposal. There is little evidence, however, that they expected to be challenged on moral grounds. A number of factors converged to transform a routine request for permission to build a pipeline into a high profile public debate. The growing self-awareness of native peoples, the emergence of well-organized environmental and native rights movements, the fact of a Liberal minority government, the enormous costs of the project in relation to questionable benefits for Canadians, the small amount of gas discovered in the North, and the growing "gas bubble" in Alberta all helped to shatter the aura of inevitability which had shrouded talk of a northern pipeline from critical public scrutiny.

The churches made a threefold contribution to the transition from inevitable next step to public debate, and to the debate once it was no longer simply taken for granted that the pipeline would be in the public interest. First, by taking the native peoples seriously they both gave added legitimacy to the natives' demand for recognition and justice and withdrew legitimacy from the dominant pattern of resource development in frontier areas. Second, by pressing ethical and religious questions the churches helped to expand the prevailing utilitarian/consequentialist framework in both deontological and ideological directions. Finally, by working together through Project North and the five dozen or so local Project North support groups the churches carried the native peoples' cry for justice to southern Canadians.

That Project North's campaigns to mobilize southern support, first for the moratorium on pipeline construction and later for constitutional rights, received little attention in this study reflects the aims of the study rather than the importance of these activities. My limited purpose has been to use the Mackenzie Valley pipeline debate as a case study in comparative ethics. I hope that someone else whose interests and talents are more historical than mine will undertake the task of telling the full story of the churches' efforts through Project North to support the rights of aboriginal peoples and to encourage all Canadians to adopt a way of life based upon conserver rather than consumer values.

Notes

1. James Gustafson, "An Analysis of Church and Society Social Ethical Writings," *Ecumenical Review*, 40, 2 (April 1988): 267-78.
2. Ibid., p. 269.
3. Project North, "A Call for a Moratorium," in *Canadian Churches and Social Justice*, ed. John R. Williams (Toronto: Anglican Book Centre and James Lorimer, 1984), p. 161.
4. Gustafson, "Analysis of Writings," p. 269.
5. Albert R. Jonsen and Stephen Toulmin, *The Abuse of Casuistry: A History of Moral Reasoning* (Berkeley and Los Angeles, California: University of California Press, 1988).
6. See Gerald Sheppard, *The Future of the Bible: Beyond Liberalism and Literalism* (Toronto: The United Church Publishing House, 1990), esp. pp. 9-20.
7. Gustafson, "Analysis of Writings," p. 273.
8. Jonsen and Toulmin, *Abuse*, p. vii.
9. Ibid., p. 271.
10. Ibid., p. 256. See also Francis Schüssler Fiorenza's discussion of retroductive warrants and reflective equilibrium in *Foundational Theology: Jesus and the Church* (New York: Crossroad, 1986).
11. I am grateful to Michael Asch and to David Goa, who interviewed Professor Asch for me in Edmonton, for their illuminating discussion of this issue.
12. Jonsen and Toulmin, *Abuse*, p. 108.
13. As I pointed out in the previous chapter, Berger claimed that his use of a metropolis-hinterland framework for his analysis of the northern economy owed more to the early work of Harold Innis than to more recent Latin American dependency theorists.
14. Darcy McKeough to Archbishop Edward Scott, April 28, 1976. General Synod Archives. Archbishop Scott's ability to explain church policies to angry lay people was related both to his pastoral skills and to his own competency as a moral theologian, i.e., as a casuist. See both his evidence submitted to the National Energy Board as a witness for the Committee for Justice and Liberty and his response under cross-examination to questions about morality and the role of scientific experts on pp. 33,384-33,395.
15. James Gustafson, *Ethics from a Theocentric Perspective, Theology and Ethics* (Chicago: University of Chicago Press 1981), p. 158. See also Charles Taylor, *Sources of the Self: The Making of Modern Identity* (Cambridge: Cambridge University Press, 1989). In his last publication delivered as lectures at Emmanuel College, Northrop Frye discussed the shift in language from description and

debate to myth and metaphor required to understand the religious dimension of life. See *The Double Vision* (Toronto: United Church Publishing House, 1990).

16.   I do not, however, want to underestimate the importance of the post-Vatican II consensus that did emerge on basic questions about the nature of the theological task and the role of the church as an agent of social transformation. For an interesting illustration of the type of theological thinking going on in ecumenical circles during the early seventies, see Patrick Kerans, S.J., "Theology of Liberation," *Social Thought* (Social Action Department of the Canadian Catholic Conference, October 1972). Kerans was at that time Director of the Social Action Department of the CCC.

17.   Ibid., p. 60

Index

SR SUPPLEMENTS

Note: Nos. 1 to 8, 10, 13, 15, 18 and 20 in this series are out of print.

STUDIES IN CHRISTIANITY AND JUDAISM / ÉTUDES SUR LE CHRISTIANISME ET LE JUDAÏSME

Note: No. 1 and Vol. 1 of No. 2 in this series are out of print.

THE STUDY OF RELIGION IN CANADA / SCIENCES RELIGIEUSES AU CANADA

DISSERTATIONS SR

EDITIONS SR

Note: Nos. 1, 3, 6 and 9 in this series are out of print.

2. *The Conception of Punishment in Early Indian Literature*
   Terence P. Day
   1982 / iv + 328 pp.

4. *Le messianisme de Louis Riel*
   Gilles Martel
   1984 / xviii + 483 p.

5. *Mythologies and Philosophies of Salvation in the Theistic Traditions of India*
   Klaus K. Klostermaier
   1984 / xvi + 552 pp.

7. *L'étude des religions dans les écoles : l'expérience américaine,
   anglaise et canadienne*
   Fernand Ouellet
   1985 / xvi + 666 p.

8. *Of God and Maxim Guns: Presbyterianism in Nigeria, 1846-1966*
   Geoffrey Johnston
   1988 / iv + 322 pp.

10. *Prometheus Rebound: The Irony of Atheism*
    Joseph C. McLelland
    1988 / xvi + 366 pp.

11. *Competition in Religious Life*
    Jay Newman
    1989 / viii + 237 pp.

12. *The Huguenots and French Opinion, 1685-1787:
    The Enlightenment Debate on Toleration*
    Geoffrey Adams
    1991 / xiv + 335 pp.

13. *Religion in History: The Word, the Idea, the Reality /
    La religion dans l'histoire : le mot, l'idée, la réalité*
    Edited by / Sous la direction de Michel Despland and/et Gérard Vallée
    1992 / x + 252 pp.

14. *Sharing Without Reckoning: Imperfect Right and the Norms of Reciprocity*
    Millard Schumaker
    1992 / xiv + 112 pp.

15. *Love and the Soul: Psychological Interpretations of the Eros and Psyche Myth*
    James Gollnick
    1992 / viii + 174 pp.

COMPARATIVE ETHICS SERIES /
COLLECTION D'ÉTHIQUE COMPARÉE

Note: No. 1 in this series is out of print.

2. *Methodist Education in Peru: Social Gospel, Politics, and American
   Ideological and Economic Penetration, 1888-1930*
   Rosa del Carmen Bruno-Jofré
   1988 / xiv + 223 pp.

3. *Prophets, Pastors and Public Choices: Canadian Churches
   and the Mackenzie Valley Pipeline Debate*
   Roger Hutchinson
   1992 / xiv + 142 pp.

Available from / en vente chez :

WILFRID LAURIER UNIVERSITY PRESS

Wilfrid Laurier University
Waterloo, Ontario, Canada   N2L 3C5

**Published for the
Canadian Corporation for Studies in Religion/
Corporation Canadienne des Sciences Religieuses
by Wilfrid Laurier University Press**